WITHDRAWN

ENFIELD LIBRARIES
9120000247303

First published in Great Britain August 2011 by Miranda Media Limited. This edition September 2011.

Copyright George Galloway 2011

The moral right of the author has been asserted

No part of this book may be used or reproduced in any manner whatsoever without written permission from the publisher except in the case of brief quotations and embodies in critical articles and reviews.

Published by Miranda Media
Printed by Imprint Digital

All photographs courtesy of, and copyright of, the Daily Record

Open Season

How Neil Lennon refused to bow down to sectarianism

George Galloway

Acknowledgements

First I must thank Ron McKay and John Wight without whose help and encouragement this book would not have been written. Wight is a writer and close political ally. McKay has been my friend for nearly 35 years - now that's a condign punishment - and he's well, simply the best (as they sing, somewhere).

And Alex Mosson (who as Glasgow's Lord Provost - the Scottish equivalent of mayor - flew the Palestinian flag from the city hall) and his ever-growing Glasgow Irish-Catholic family took me to their collective bosom nearly 30 years ago and never let go of me, through thick and thin.

Brian Dempsey, my friend and the Godfather of my grandchildren, led the rebellion which saved Celtic from ruin and gave me a fine grandstand seat at some of Celtic's greatest moments.

The late Ian Findlay introduced me to the Jungle - the concrete heartland of the Celtic support now demolished but never forgotten - the comradeship of whom will stay with me forever. Celtic's Lisbon Lions who brought home the European Cup to Britain for the very first time, every one of whom was born within a 30-mile radius of the club's stadium, achieving something which will never be matched. Big Jock Stein knew how to make himself and his football team, immortal.

To Father Noel Barry for many years of good fellowship and to the Mullens, a cool Celtic tribe by the Atlantic.

The Daily Record, its editor Bruce Waddell and those staffers who make my writing look better than it is in my weekly column there, and their picture desk, whose cracking images hopefully illuminate this book and make it a keepsake. Particularly to Record picture guru Brian Gallagher.

To Bob Wylie for proving that being a Hun doesn't have to mean having a square head or a hard heart.

My maternal grandparents Thomas O'Reilly and Annie Dougan for giving me the Celtic gene, Jimmy Divers for running the supporters bus from Lochee, Neilly Mochan the first Celtic player I ever met, my late father George Galloway for teaching me to play and to love football, my mother, Sheila Reilly, for making me a Tim and my son Zein Galloway whose Celtic pyjamas are, well, the cat's PJs.

And to every Celtic man or woman I ever met along the way to Paradise. Hail Hail The Celts are here!

George Galloway
London, the close season of 2011

London Borough of Enfield	
91200000247303	
Askews & Holts	Jan-2012
920	£10.00

Bhoys will be bhoys: managers past and present

'I decided to write this book when I saw
the Glasgow Celtic Football Club manager
Neil Lennon being attacked
at Tynecastle in May 2011.
It was the last straw.'

George Galloway, July 2011

In the beginning

I'd cried foul about sectarianism before of course, as a Scottish Member of Parliament for 18 of my 23 years, in my Daily Record column, on my TalkSport radio show (hundreds of thousands of people have listened on YouTube to my clashes with bigots on the radio), even on television - Press TV - no doubt to the general bemusement of my international audience there. Surely not, they must have said. Surely not in Scotland in 2011, could a football manager be sent live bombs in the post, bullets too, and over and over.

Surely not, in Scotland in 2011, could a football manager's wife and their child hunker down under police protection, her finger poised over a panic button. The walls of her house and even the road outside daubed with painted threats to wade in her family's blood. But it surely was, all that and much more.

I wrote a short piece which said that if Neil Lennon walked away from Scotland over all this, the country would die of shame. He didn't and we're still alive. But the shame remains, ours. The shame of hating a man because of the job he does in football. The shame of blaming the man, the victim, for what happened to him. For the proud way he holds himself. Or on his unwillingness to cringe. For his unflinching Irishness and fidelity to his Roman Catholic faith. The half-spoken sub-text that if he'd only lower his eyes when he's talking, reaction to him would be less vindictive. That it was really his fault not Scotland's.

Gradually Neil Lennon took on a Malcolm X persona to me. Brave, dignified, unbroken. And as Malcolm said, 'if you don't stand for something, you'll fall for anything'. And many have fallen for those self-serving myths. That Lennon is to blame. That Scotland is 'one country, many cultures'. That it's the 'greatest wee country in the world'.

Large parts of Scotland remain in denial about what really lies beneath this story, anti-Catholic sectarianism and anti-Irish racism. And that the answer is not, in Malcolm X's famous words, for the Catholic Irish to behave like 'house niggers', the Gone With the Wind stereotype slaves whose docility won them a place at the masters' table. But only to serve there.

Again in Malcolm's words, 'Being at the table doesn't make you a diner, unless you eat some of what's on the plates. Being here in America doesn't make you an American. Being born here in America doesn't make you an American.'

The answer, after at least 150 years of this is to stand up tall and say, enough of this. We are equal citizens here. We are not going anywhere. We will not tolerate this any longer.

We are not ashamed, and we are not afraid. Our day has come.

This book is dedicated to the maternal side of my own family who came to Scotland as Irish, Catholic, immigrants. The O'Reillys, the Dougans, the Floods, the Feeneys.

They arrived, barefoot, in cattle boats at Anderston Quay in Glasgow, and some of them lived long enough to see me represent the area in the British parliament. They walked the road and the miles to Dundee and toiled from six in the morning to six at night in the jute and flax mills upon which the city was built. The mill-owners, 'fairly mak ye work for yer 10 shillings and 54 pence;' in the words of Dundee's poet Mary Brooksbank.

They lived in Lochee, where I was born and raised in an attic at 12a Atholl Street. The area was known as Tipperary on account of the teeming Irish immigrant population living in the slums there, within walking distance of the mills. I've come a long way from Tipperary. But it's never left me.

In this book I will tell the story of the hatred, racism, bigotry and even attempted acts of terrorism to which Neil Lennon has been subjected. I will debunk the kind of self-serving mythology which has surrounded his ordeal. That, 'he brings it upon himself'. That 'both sides' are 'as bad as each other'. That it's 'only a minority'. That Scotland is otherwise a tolerant inclusive country of many cultures, all equal and equally welcome. That if only Lennon didn't strut so, if only he'd lower his eyes when he addresses us. If he wasn't, as Bob Dylan described Ruben 'Hurricane' Carter, 'such a craaazy nigger'. But a 'house nigger instead'. Meek mild accepting.

Knowing his place.

And I will place the story where it belongs, in the context of a chronic, centuries-old Scottish bigotry against Catholics, Irish Catholics in particular. Having no time to re-invent the wheel, nor any wish to, I will draw with suitable attribution I hope on the work of peerless academics like Tom Devine and others who have established beyond peradventure the existence of this racism and sectarianism. And I will give the reader some of my own experience in this field too.

Which started early in my public life. It always amazed me that bigots took such pains to establish who we 'Fenians' were. In my case not having attended a Catholic school I didn't have the ashes on my forehead quite so early as some.

But even in the Labour party, a party which in my early days in politics, and to a lesser extent still today, commanded the allegiance of the great majority of Scotland's Roman Catholic voters it was there lying in the undergrowth like a snake.

Councillor Sam Campbell, for example, was one of the most powerful of Scotland's local government Dons. Dapper, trim, oozing authority, the Lothians' powerbroker growled in my ear at a Labour conference one year, apropos of absolutely nothing, 'Oh Georgie....ye never telt me ye were a wee Fenian!'.

I had never 'telt' him otherwise, or anything at all. I had never spoken to him in my life at that point. I was only about 21 years old and hardly worth even noticing for a man like him. But he'd quite clearly done the genealogy.

In the general election of 1987 at which I was first elected I was atop an open top bus (a regular place to find me at election times) in Glasgow's Byres Road, parked up near a posh delicatessen in what is the centre of the city's West End. I was speaking into a microphone when I became aware of a middle-aged, middle class lady in a Royal blue coat with white piping (later this would have been a giveaway) who was cupping her hand and shouting something up at me which I could not hear.

When I stopped speaking I lent over the top of the bus and cupped my ear.

'We know what you are,' she shouted.

Thinking she was a, 'Why don't you go back to Russia?' type who regarded me as a 'Commie' I shouted back., 'And what am I?'.

To my amazement, out of that fine mouth, and in a Glasgow West End Kelvinside accent, she shouted, 'You're nothing but a Fenian bastard!'.

My mother who was standing next to me at the time was offended by at least the second word.

'He might be a Fenian but I assure you he's no

bastard!' she retorted

Some people in the constituency never accepted me as their MP. I used to hold my constituency surgeries in Partick Burgh Hall but had to move them because this required me to move through some 'no-go' streets and more than once I had threats of violence against me in my first years in parliament.

In fact so many threats were delivered to me in Glasgow that I was virtually assigned my own Special Branch officers who regularly visited me, advised me, and from time to time protected me. They were fine officers who always did their duty but let's just say I was aware that sometimes that they probably thought that lady in Byres Road had a point!

Eventually Strathclyde Police allocated me an officer, after an actual assault upon me, a detective by the name of Joseph Cahill, who as the name suggests was more simpatico. So simpatico that he later married my close friend and protege Pauline McNeill, who for a long time was the member of the Scottish Parliament for my constituency. Joe is now a prominent advocate in the High Court.

The cause of most of my troubles on that front were my views on Ireland. I have all my life supported the struggle for freedom, unity and independence in Ireland. This is in my DNA but it's not mere sentiment. Ireland was England's first colony. She was taken by force. When force was no longer enough she was cheated of the independence she voted for by the partition of the country, the gerrymandering of what is described as 'Ulster' to ensure a permanent (so they hoped) Protestant (mainly settlers from Scotland), 'Unionist' majority. I hate colonialism, not for religious or familial reasons, but because I am above all an anti-imperialist.

Once I came home from school having been presented by a huge map of the world coloured largely in pink, and told my Irish grandfather Tommy Reilly (the family dropped the O' when they came to Scotland. He was in fact the illegitimate son of the baronial grandfather of Sir Tony O'Reilly, the multi-millionaire newspaper magnate and rugby hero. Close Tony, but it doesn't entitle you to any of my money!) that the teacher had told us that, 'Britain had an empire so vast that upon it the sun never set'

My grandfather answered, 'that's because God would never trust the British in the dark'.

This stand on Ireland could have been known by any of my constituents through my membership of 'Time to Go' led by ex-minister Clare Short and many public statements I had made over the years.

But it probably didn't come home to most of them until they saw the front page of the Sun newspaper - the UK edition, this was before there was a Scottish edition - which contained a single large photograph, of me, and a single large word in a big, black, bold headline. TRAITOR.

It was in 1990 and I had just marched through the streets of Dublin on a Time to Go demonstration. With Gerry Adams and Martin McGuiness who then had none of the titles and such 'respectability' as they surely have today.

I appeared on the back of a lorry with the duo, and listened whilst a bald and beautiful Sinead O'Connor sang Bobby Sands', 'I wish I was back home in Derry' from the back of the truck.

It was in retrospect a bolder thing to do than I had thought at the time. I was in no doubt by the Monday morning and the Sun on my breakfast table portended dark clouds to come for sure.

For the next 15 years the local Orange walks - there were several Orange halls in my constituency - would stop right outside my window in Anderston, birthplace of Billy Connolly and then a significantly Irish part of the city, and beat their Lambeg drums until they were sure they had shaken me from my bed (unknown to them I love the sound of a Lambeg drum). But that was the least of my worries.

In the subsequent general election in 1992 I woke up on polling day to discover literally thousands of green and white sticky-backed A4 posters bearing the legend 'Galloway = IRA' had been posted throughout the constituency. Outside every polling station. On every bus shelter. In fact more of them than we could count.

I doubled my majority.

The following Saturday at Celtic Park several of

them were being brandished aloft in what was known as the Jungle - the heartland part of the stadium.

It was the first time I'd been branded a traitor in the British press. But not, of course, the last. But I was right. And just like on all the subsequent findings of treason, proud of the stand I had taken. But of course the prouder you are the more they hate you. Which brings me back to Neil Lennon...

I was flying to Glasgow to perform a one-man show at the Royal Concert Hall. A mixture of comedy, politics, personal anecdotes, even the occasional song! I had performed hundreds of these, 'An evening with George Galloway MP', including a highly-successful show in the Gorbals' Citizens Theatre. A politician who could get people to pay money to hear him speak, I was then!

This show turned out to be different. I was sat, as was then my wont, on BA flights in the front row aisle seat. Normally I didn't have luggage and this usually ensured a quick exit from the airport.

This time I was carrying a big bag of books for sale after the event and the bag was in the hold. A number of rough-looking men began boarding the flight in ones and twos. I began to be aware of first baleful stares then muttered imprecations in my direction as they went by me to take their seats. Once ensconced and emboldened by their numbers my fellow passengers began hurling insults and even tossing the odd rolled up piece of paper. Foolishly I did not ask for the pilot to call ahead and ensure a police presence at Glasgow Airport. I soon wished I had.

I was off the plane like a shot and headed for the baggage hall, hoping against hope that the posse behind me were travelling light. They were not. Soon the baggage hall was full of, more or less, them and me.

Their leader came up to an inch from my face, so close I could smell the rancid beer on his breath. 'I'd like to knock you down, but my religion doesn't allow it,' he said, unconvincingly.

'Why?' I asked lamely.

'Because of your newspaper columns,' he replied to my surprise. I write a weekly column for the Daily Record, known by many (though not by me) as the Daily Ranger. I write about issues which might have concerned my religiously-circumscribed, would-be assailant only infrequently. Conscious of Scotland's demographics the paper would prefer me to steer a wide berth on such matters. They've never censored me nor even told me that explicitly, I just know it to be true.

I have no idea which of my columns he and his friends had taken exception to but I was sure it wasn't my views on the situation in Abkhazia even before I saw the music cases start to come onto the baggage carousel. They were an Orange band! By then, less religiously restrained boots were kicking me, first on the ankles then on the calves now on the shins. At one point both of my feet were being stood on, hard. Then a beer belly tried to bounce me onto the carousel. I worked out that they were neither punching me nor applying the famous Glasgow kiss (the head-butt, a curiously Scottish form of assault) so as to try and avoid the CCTV. Anyway the blows were now coming in so thick and fast that I honestly began to fear the plunge of cold steel in my back.

I was conscious, as a man not known for being a shrinking violet, of the need to maintain my dignity. And as a public man of the special danger of humiliation, at least, in which I now stood. There were too many of them to fight back. So I made a dash for a small office off the baggage hall and told the BAA employee there to call the police. I took the phone and spoke to the police myself.

'This is George Galloway the MP,' I said 'I'm in danger in the baggage hall at Glasgow Airport, I have been assaulted and I'm in fear of my life'.

It took Strathclyde's finest 10 full minutes to arrive. In an international airport. If the flautists and drummers had wanted to they could have given me a thorough hiding and then had time to have a coffee in Starbucks before safely departing the premises.

The police took me to their prefabricated headquarters across the road and took my statement. As I was explaining the sectarian nature of the abuse I had taken another officer came in to say that CCTV outside the airport had shown a coach picking the men up outside and driving them off. They were returning from an Orange walk in London, the officer told me. It was your bad luck to have been on the same flight, he said.

Even worse luck, the chief constable later told me as he explained why the men who had been identified from their block booking, had not been charged – 'there is no CCTV in the baggage hall.'

Not long afterwards the international airport was breached by terrorist fanatics with the greatest of ease. They blew themselves up after being heroically fought by passengers and airport staff.

Just as well they hadn't known the baggage hall area was a security black hole.

As I actually knew that a cloud no bigger than a man's hand can be the harbinger of great storms to come it is surprising in retrospect that I was not more alarmed when my long-time ally Ron McKay told me he needed to talk to me urgently about the colour green.

McKay was acting as my election agent when I made an ill-conceived bid for the Holyrood parliament, standing for the City of Glasgow in May 2011. It was ill-conceived for a number of reasons. I totally underestimated the difficulties of a miniscule party in surviving the crush between the Scottish juggernauts of Labour and the SNP. I under-estimated the electoral handicap it would represent in declaring, from the start, that if elected I would back Labour to form a government and never support the SNP (though I could in conscience have said no other).

I over-estimated how keen the Scottish media would be to see me elected – if only to brighten their professional lives – and how my quite well-ensconced friends therein would be able to keep me visible to the electorate. I under-estimated the extent of the wreckage in Scottish left-wing politics caused by the Tommy Sheridan v News of the World affair and how I might be damaged by my high-profile support for Tommy in that battle (again in conscience I could do no other). I thought I could raise more money, more active supporters and of course, get more votes than I actually did.

All in all it turned into a bit of an embarrassment. Sure, I beat the Liberal-Democrats. But that's not the achievement it once was. I was runner-up for the last Glasgow seat, but a long way behind. I got nearly seven thousand votes, but I would have needed about 10,500. And the whole thing cost me a fortune, especially as I had to give up almost my entire income for around seven weeks whilst shelling out mightily around the city during the campaign. Now that I come to think of it...it had been McKay's idea that I should stand!

Anyway, I knew that in the old days of the British occupation of all of Ireland (as opposed to the current occupation of the Six Counties) they'd been, 'hangin' men and women, for the wearin' o' the green'. The song is probably metaphorical but you know what I mean. What on earth could McKay mean, though, when he said we had a problem over the colour green?

I soon found out as he arrived, grim-faced.

'Our election address' he said, 'there's a mutiny over the use of the colour green'.

I must say I laughed out loud, but he didn't see the funny side as he'd been the one arguing the toss with the greenophobes.

Against my better judgement I had agreed to run in the election not as an individual like the redoubtable Margo MacDonald in Edinburgh (which would in retrospect have been the better thing to do) but in joint harness with a collection of far-left groups who would have had to stand in their own right otherwise. These included, of course, Solidarity - Tommy's party - and the Socialist Workers' Party, which turned out to have precious few workers and by the end of the campaign was not even really a party at all.

I headed a list entitled The Respect Party (George Galloway) - Coalition Against Cuts. Apart from being a hell of a mouthful this alphabet soup ensured me a place third from the bottom of an enormously long ballot paper which turned out to be another electoral liability (amongst several).

In the weeks running up to the decision I had to balance what these parties would bring to the table (Tommy, whom I still love dearly whatever they say he's done, promised me a hundred activists - in the end I didn't see more than a dozen) with the loss of independent control of the political messages, campaign strategy and tactics etc which such an alliance implied.

This mistake cannot be blamed on McKay or anyone else though. This decision was mine alone. In mitigation I plead that it could have been worse. I actually fell out with Tommy, just before he entered Barlinnie Prison to begin his prison sentence, for the one and only time in the 25 years I've known him.

Tommy pressed me to take his wife Gail as my running mate - placing her as number two, after me, at the head of the list. Although I have been friendly with Gail since long before she married Tommy - she'd been the stewardess on my regular BA flight to and from London through most of the near 20 years I was a Westminster MP from the city - and sympathised greatly with her predicament, I refused.

'That would make my electoral campaign effectively a referendum about you,' I told Tommy. It was one of the only judgments I got right in the whole failed campaign.

I did promise that if I was elected I would hire Gail Sheridan as my PA, and of course I would have kept that promise. For some though that was not enough. An official of the Fire Brigades Union in Scotland, Kenny Ross, who heads up the Defend Tommy Sheridan Campaign, repeatedly pressed me to go and visit Tommy in the jail, during the election campaign. When I finally told him that I would do so, but after polling day, I never heard from him again. Mind you the same thing happened after he had promised me a fire engine to lead one of my caravans into Gaza.

A few days before polling day his union announced they were backing the candidate of the Green Party against me.

Ah now, speaking of the colour green..!

'The Trots are insisting that the election address must not be in green,' said Ron McKay, 'any other colour but green, they say'.

This was peculiar on several levels. First, Respect, whose campaign this officially was, did everything in green and red. But so did Solidarity! And what's wrong with green in any case?

'Well, they say that it is possible the colour choice could subliminally send out a sectarian message' said an exasperated McKay. 'I've told them to fuck off, but it just won't go away, and so I promised I'd put the matter in front of you' (me being the lead candidate and just as importantly the man who was paying for half a million of the damn things).

'But anybody who might consider voting for me if only my leaflet wasn't in green is the kind of bigot who a) doesn't exist and b) we don't want' I exploded.

This argument continued over several crucial days and involved the man from Solidarity (whose own colours were green), the man from the Socialist Workers' Party (whose party split a few days later in the middle of the campaign leaving him with a handful of members as the brightest, best and most active of his comrades went off to form yet another socialist party) and above all the man from the Socialist Party

(Scotland) – I know it's confusing but try to keep up

Eventually I pulled rank (financial as well as political) and green it was (even though some argued until they were, er, blue in the face!). A shade which was about to become more significant.

The crescendo of violence and threats against Neil Lennon coincided with my attempt to be elected to the Scottish parliament in the spring and early summer of 2011. And the climax of maybe the most controversial Scottish football season ever.

I was in a rising state of indignation, feeling every cut the bigots sought to inflict on him, every jibe that was hurled in Lennon's direction. And fury at the tone of political and journalistic 'even-handedness' which at first at least accompanied the swelling of the tide – some of which coverage came close to blaming the victim.

An e-mail arrived from a friend now working in the Bahamas and, of course, an official of the Celtic Supporters Club there. 'We need a demonstration George, and you are the only one who can lead us.'

It was one of those Eureka! moments. I was lying in bed in the early morning at the apartment overlooking the river of my close friend Brian Dempsey, the man who led the rebels in the war to save Celtic from the old biscuit-tin board. The man who got to announce – 'The war is over, the rebels have won'.

I sat bolt-upright in bed and began to text and call my closest colleagues and plan the next move. Within a couple of hours I was in Glasgow's Hilton Hotel with Ron McKay, John Wight, Jim Lister a long-time ally in the Palestinian struggle and fellow Celtic man who stages events for a living, Brian Dempsey and Neil Lennon's lawyer Paul McBride QC.

As the situation was moving fast - I had been warned by the anti-terrorist branch of Strathclyde Police that I might be a target, Paul had already been sent a bomb in the post, Neil was, it seemed, open season, and Trish Godman one of the presiding officers of the Scottish parliament had received a bomb too, just for wearing a Celtic top on her last day as a member of the Scottish parliament. We had to move fast.

For me it was natural to stand up openly publicly and militantly in support of the victims of sectarian attack. The fact that I was myself from the same background as the victims made no difference to me. If the victims had been Jews, Muslims, gays, whomever or whatever, I would have felt and proposed to do the same. If I were the only person saying and doing so, that wouldn't matter to me either. One thing I would NEVER do is refrain from standing up because it might upset the perpetrators. Or those from whence they sprang and who had not yet been won to disavow them. In other words I wanted action in solidarity with Irish Catholic victims of sectarianism in Scotland –

whether Scotland's non-Catholics liked it or not.

Of course I hoped that the vast majority of them would like it and I remain convinced that they would. But they could have no veto on what, where and when was done in solidarity with the victims.

In our gathering we proposed not a march but a rally, in George Square in Glasgow's city centre. I had filled George Square, against the machine once before – and without the benefit of mobile phones and the internet which hadn't reached Glasgow by 1992!

In the aftermath – in fact the morning after – of the Doomsday of John Major's Tory victory that year, when the Tories were wiped out in Scotland but returned, their faces set against Home Rule, in England, myself then the MP for Glasgow Kelvin, the late and lamented Bill Speirs from the Scottish TUC, Dennis Canavan MP, John McAllion MP, Willie McKelvey MP, Irene Adams MP (now in the House of Lords), Stuart Cosgrove (who became famous as Tam Cowan's amanuensis), Gordon McDougall (now a top honcho at STV), Ricky Ross, Pat Kane, Fish and others from the worlds of entertainment, politics and trades' unionism formed Scotland United – the name was suggested by Canavan – to demand a multi-option referendum on Scotland's future.

That was on the Friday morning. We announced it during exhausted television interviews throughout that day amidst the sea of sadness in Scotland at the Tory victory but we couldn't know if we were being heard.

We leafleted the pubs and student unions on the Friday night with just another A5 leaflet (in the wake of millions of such leaflets over the preceding four weeks) and Parkhead on the Saturday afternoon.

On the Sunday, the day of the rally, the sun shone all day as we drove an open-topped bus onto the square to act as the platform. The speakers clambered aboard early to discuss the speaking order and test the equipment. There was a slip of a girl called Nicola Sturgeon from the Youth SNP – now the highly rated deputy leader of Scotland's governing party.

There were the usual Labour movement suspects. But most importantly when we got back on the bus for real there were tens of thousands of people in the square. We had filled it, without Twitter, Facebook, YouTube, without adverts without posters....we had filled George Square full of mainly young people, excited not exhausted, determined not depressed.

Well I thought it was a good enough cause – the cause of Neil Lennon and everything this story signified – to try and fill George Square again.

We contacted the council and squared the officials there. We planned to ask the city's Lord Provost Bob Winter – a good Celtic man too – to preside, partly to smooth any potential problems with the owners of the square. We drafted an invitation to Alex Salmond, the chief minister, to his New Labour opposite number, indeed the leaders of all the parties. We drafted an invitation letter to Walter Smith, coming to the end of his last season as Rangers greatest-ever manager and who had helped me get elected in Glasgow twice before.

I decided to call the event - Scotland United Against Sectarianism And Bigotry.

There already is a Scotland United, pointed out a young whippersnapper present – it's run by Aamer Anwar. I'm a founder member of Scotland United, I said, I was one of its leaders. There can be no copyright on the title Scotland United, certainly not when you've added the words against sectarianism and bigotry.

For many years I had employed as my assistant a talented young man by the name of David Moxham. He had been unemployed when I met him and a little down on his luck. But I recognised his abilities and we become extremely close, even regularly holidaying together. After my expulsion from New Labour over the Iraq War and the abolition of my Glasgow constituency (just in case!) Moxham informed me that he was going to apply for a job at the Scottish TUC. Although it was a blow personally I gave him my blessing, telling him truthfully, that I had always felt he was cut out for greater things.

We parted amicably and although I was surprised at his apparent inattention to the subsequent upheavals in my life – good and bad – I had no reason to believe that he, again a Celtic supporter, would have any problem with what I had in mind. So I asked him to try and bring the STUC on board and if he couldn't then to speak at the rally in a personal capacity – something he has regularly done on other platforms. For the avoidance of doubt I told him that I really needed him to do this for me. Blood is thicker than water, I thought.

Nine days before the rally I was asked for a meeting to discuss it, because of anxieties from a quite unlikely quarter. The Trotskyite Socialist Workers' Party.

Now I'd had my problems with the SWP before – although I was back in harness with them in the Scottish elections, at least as part of the Coalition Against Cuts, the banner under which I was standing. But it honestly never occurred to me for a second that the 'Revolutionary Party' as they style themselves could possibly have any 'anxieties' about a rally in defence of Neil Lennon.

It's true that just days before this request for a discussion on this the SWP in Glasgow had split not just in two – the vast majority of the party's youngest and best activists had resigned as part of some typical far-left wrangle, though both parts remained nominally committed to my campaign. So it may be that the SWP leader of the rump in Glasgow, Jimmy Ross, was in the middle of a kind of political nervous breakdown over these extraneous matters but when we sat down in the cafe of the Tron Theatre in Glasgow's Trongate he addressed me as if we had reached some dread, profound political juncture.

He said that the SWP were extremely worried about my proposed rally because 'it would likely only attract Catholics'. That it would be 'divisive within the working class' and could only go ahead (with their blessing at least) if the STUC officially backed it, if the main political parties backed it, if it had 'senior Rangers figures' involved as well as churchmen of the Protestant stripe.

I was stunned into silence momentarily. A void which was quickly filled by John Wight and Ron McKay who practically exploded out of their seats.

'If a fuckin' asylum seeker in Sighthill had been sent a parcel bomb you'd call a fuckin' demonstration at the drop of a leaflet, ya cowardly bastard,' said McKay, controlling his anger, relatively.

'You wouldn't wait for white people from every political organisation to line up before you'd call it – you'd call it and trust that they'd have to get on board! And if they didn't you'd call it anyway. Why is it different for Catholics?' McKay demanded.

Trying to be the voice of reason I more quietly explained the following. I intended to invite the leaders of all the parties. But if they wouldn't come, shame on them. It couldn't be a reason for not going ahead. I did intend to invite Walter Smith. But ditto. If he didn't come that could not veto the rally. I had, I said, approached David Moxham, my old pal at the STUC. I was sure that he would try and get the unions on board but that if he could not then I was even more sure he would speak in a personal capacity. At least for old times sake.

And lastly, I had asked Aamer Anwar, of 'Scotland United', whose organisation itself had wide affiliation, including the STUC, to be the co-chair and to absorb some of what I was sure would be the credit for a timely and important and successful initiative.

After a very tense, almost surreal, hour or so trying to talk a 'revolutionary leader' down off the ledge of abstention from the struggle I left the SWP-ers to discuss the matter amongst themselves. I never heard a word from them again. It was worse, much worse than that.

The next day Sunday I wrote my column for the Monday morning Daily Record announcing the Scotland United Against Sectarianism And Bigotry rally the following Monday in George Square. The Record laid it out beautifully with a frieze of photographs of leaders of Scotland United photographs below a clarion call to rally against sectarianism. It even gave the time people should turn up.

At least in the first, non-Glasgow edition.

By the time of the second edition one of my erstwhile colleagues had phoned up the Record and got the date and time of the rally removed from the paper. They told the night editor that these were my wishes too. That the date had been changed and that we'd all look foolish if the print run continued as it was.

The next morning Glasgow's top Trot explained

that 'everybody' was against the rally going ahead as planned. That Aamer Anwar was against it. That David Moxham was against it. 'We can't have a Catholic rally in Glasgow,' said the stolidly anti-racist SWP figure, Ross.

Even when they're being bombed through the post, he didn't add.

Ross claimed that Anwar had texted me explaining why he was pulling out. I phoned Anwar, several times. I texted him. He texted me back saying he would be in touch later, that he was, 'out with his family'.

Finally I spoke to Anwar. He explained, well every reason Ross had been against the rally actually. Word for word. He claimed to have texted me all this. I told him I had received no such text (I did receive it, 72 hours after he claimed to have sent it – I've kept it for posterity).

He didn't deny that he had been involved in the sabotage of my Daily Record column. Moreover he told me that he had phoned Moxham – who never contacted me again by the way – and persuaded him against the rally and even that he'd phoned Paul McBride QC in South Africa to do the same with him. All this without a single word to me.

If the above sounds bitter then that's because I am bitter, not just at the scale and source of the personal betrayal involved.

But much more importantly because I believe the

whole story demonstrates the total ambivalence which exists in Scotland and in all corners about anti-Catholic bigotry and anti-Irish racism.

Not only bitter where Aamer Anwar was concerned, I was saddened. He and I went back quite a few years and had worked closely together in a number of campaigns. I'd always admired his willingness to stand up and be counted as a Muslim during a climate of hostility towards Muslims without fear or favour, whether as a lawyer in the courts or as a leading activist in the streets.

Indeed, if Neil Lennon had been a Muslim, George Square would have filled on May 2, 2011, the day of the anti-sectarianism rally that never happened; the rally that was cancelled by 'the revolutionary left' for fear of upsetting people.

Aamer Anwar was clearly unrepentant. He and Ron McKay had a bitter shouting match on the steps of the Strathclyde University union just days before the mooted and then aborted rally, which culminated in Aamer declaring, as he stormed off, 'I don't give a fuck what Galloway thinks'.

Many weeks after I had folded my tent and slunk out of Glasgow my tail well and truly between my legs one of my closest colleagues Rob Hoveman met up with SWP grandee and retired Glasgow University professor Mike Gonzalez (whose involvement in the entire Glasgow election campaign could've filled the back of an entire postage stamp). In the rarefied surroundings of London's Bloomsbury Gonzalez opined that, 'Galloway made a big mistake in the election campaign'.

'How, so?' asked Hoveman, 'What mistake?'

'Well', said the good professor, 'planning that sectarian rally for a start.'

'Don't you mean ANTI-Sectarian rally?' asked Hoveman.

With logic worthy of Hegel himself Gonzalez shot back, 'An anti-sectarian rally in which only one sect takes part becomes a sectarian rally!'

So there you have it, my efforts to organise a rally against sectarianism have become an attempt to have a sectarian rally. As the use of green in my election leaflets had become a crime against the people – likely to divide the 'working class'.

Hail Hail.

Ireland's scottish problem

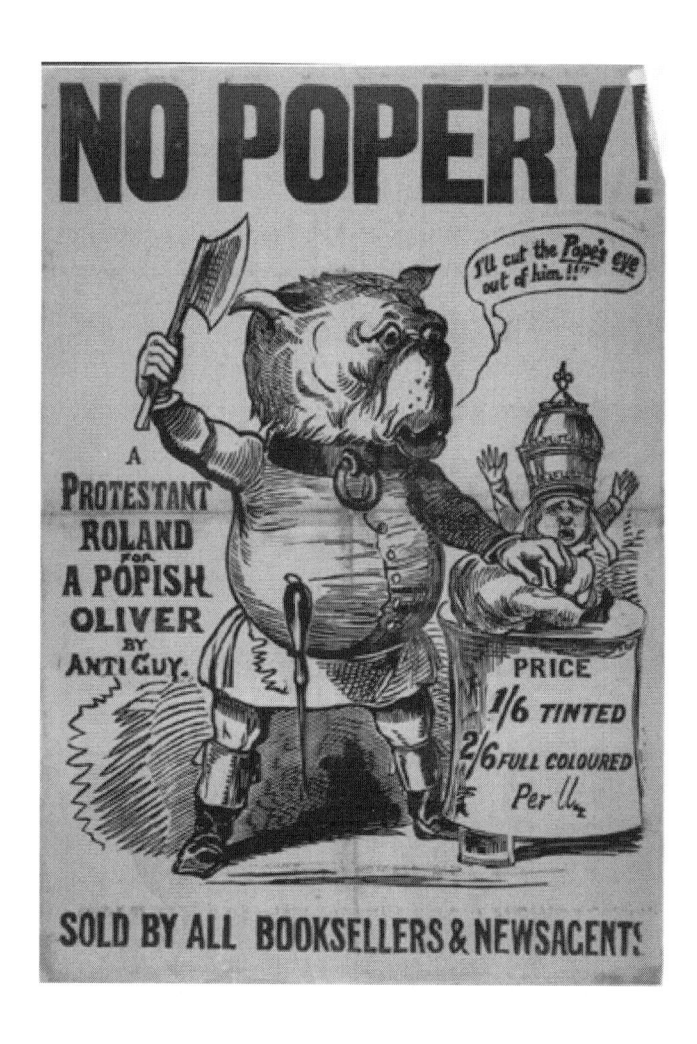

Anti-Irish Catholic racism and bigotry has been embedded within Scottish society since Irish Catholic immigrants first arrived in the country at the beginning of the 19th century.

Prior to 1830 some 6-8,000 would make the journey to Scotland each year, most on a temporary basis to find work during harvest season, and many of those from across the border in England.

In line with Scotland's rapid industrialisation throughout the mid to latter part of the 19th century, the Irish soon began to arrive and settle permanently as a source of cheap labour in the great shipyards on the Clyde, as well as down the mines and in the steel plants and textile factories that cemented Scotland's international reputation as the workshop of the world.

It was estimated that by the mid 19th Century around three-quarters of all the labourers working on the docks throughout mainland Britain were Irish, along with two-thirds of all those working down the mines and almost half the female workers in the textile mills of Greenock. Although Glasgow and the west of Scotland were the main destinations for Irish immigrants, due to the proximity of that part of the country to Ireland and the heavy industry located there, an Irish presence also emerged in Dundee, attracted by the textile and jute mills that sprang up around the same period, but also in the whaling and shipyards which by then in operation on the Tay. My own relatives, the O'Reillys, the Dougans, the Floods were among the Irish families which settled there.

Edinburgh also acquired its own Irish immigrant community that was again used as a source of cheap labour, here in the dockyards around the port of Leith but also in the tanneries and mills that were then located in the city's Old Town. Indeed, the capital's Irish population settled in this part of the city to such an extent that the Canongate and Cowgate soon became known as Little Ireland. Similarly, in my own home city of Dundee there was an Irish quarter called Lochee in which I was born and lived the first years of my life which was known colloquially as Tipperary.

Today Edinburgh's Old Town is home to those who can afford the extortionate prices and rents of upmarket residential flats. It is also a magnet for tourists and visitors from all over the world, attracted by the Old Town's abundant history and culture, with a liberal sprinkling of boutique hotels, restaurants, bars and nightclubs also making it a prime destination for revellers each and every weekend.

As a result it is hard to imagine that this part of the city was once a disease-ridden, rat-infested hovel, where the city's Irish immigrants lived in squalor in rundown and overcrowded tenements, disdained by a society that was happy to exploit their labour while at the same time scorning the very ground upon which they walked.

Incidentally, one of Ireland's greatest sons, James

Connolly, was born in Edinburgh in 1868, with a plaque marking the very tenement in the city's Cowgate where he took his first breath. He took his last breath of course in Kilmainham jail strapped to a chair, whereupon he was executed by the British Empire - but I mustn't get ahead of myself.

The economic migration from Ireland of the early to mid 19th Century was replaced by a veritable flood of refugees seeking escape from the Great Potato Famine that devastated Britain's first and last colony between 1845 and 1852. Approximately a million perished and another million emigrated as a result, while Britain's ruling and political classes wrung their hands in obeisance to that fundamentalist religion known as Free Trade.

The French call it *laissez faire*. I prefer to call it genocide.

By the end of it Ireland's population had been decimated, shrunk by 20 per cent and its impact condemned the country to a century of underdevelopment, particularly in the south, while the rest of Europe boomed on the back of mass industrialisation. In the words of Brigadier General Thomas F Meagher of the famed Irish Brigade of the great Army of the Potomac, which fought to destroy the Confederacy and end slavery in the United States: 'The sword of famine is less sparing than the bayonet of the soldier.'

In Scotland the Irish population increased by 90 per

cent in just seven years to just over 200,000, or 7.2 per cent of the total population.

The Irish were never treated as anything other than an alien presence in their adopted land; their culture, native language and religion a stain on the fabric of an otherwise unblemished and pure Protestant utopia. This was the period during which NINA (No Irish Need Apply) signs were prevalent in newspaper advertisements for jobs and accommodation, and when Presbyterian ministers used the pulpit to spout anti-Popery diatribes that were designed to sow fear and foment anti-Irish Catholic sentiment across the land. Indeed, as late as the 1920s the Church of Scotland could still publish a pamphlet titled, *'The Menace of the Irish race to our Scottish Nationality'*.

HELP WANTED
NO IRISH NEED APPLY

Such were the pitiful living conditions of Irish Catholics in Scotland by the latter part of the 19th Century, and such was the extent of the social apartheid they endured, the Catholic Church stepped in to provide social services and organise a network of soup kitchens and other charitable services without which thousands more would have perished from poverty than actually did.

It was common currency to blame the squalor in which Irish Catholic immigrants lived on the alcoholism that was rife among them. But here we have a classic case of blame the victim, the bread and butter of racists and bigots throughout history. The truth is that alcoholism wasn't to blame for the squalor and poverty of Irish immigrant communities in Scotland. Rather it was the squalor and poverty they were living in that was to blame for the spread of alcoholism.

The conditions being suffered by Irish Catholic immigrants to Scotland was in marked contrast to the fortunes of Irish Protestant immigrants, who came to Scotland predominately from the North. Their arrival, mostly in the latter half of the 19th Century, introduced the anti-Catholic doctrine of Orangeism to Scotland, and soon exercised a cultural influence that remains significant to this day. Unsurprisingly, both economically and socially the assimilation into Scottish society of those Irish Protestant immigrants was comparatively smooth and pain free.

Tensions among working class Protestant and Irish Catholics were exacerbated by the way that employers were allowed to exploit the influx of Irish immigrant labour to push down wages, which Protestant workers blamed on their Irish Catholic counterparts. But workers don't force wages down, employers do, and preventing them doing so requires solidarity between workers regardless of religious, ethnic or cultural differences.

In Scotland, especially the west of the country, prospects for such class solidarity were impeded by the pandering of many Scottish workers to anti-Irish racism and anti Catholic bigotry, a state of affairs that suited the interests of the bosses and employers.

The dawn of Celtic pride

Around this time the setting up of football clubs to meet the need for a social identity and sense of belonging among Scotland's Irish Catholic communities began in line with the growing popularity of the sport among the working class in general. And the first tender steps towards the creation of organised leagues and competitions for the new clubs that were springing up were being taken. Hibernian, derived from the Roman name for Ireland *Hibernia*, were formed in Edinburgh in 1875 by the city's Irish immigrants, with none other than James Connolly an early fan of a club. Adopting the colours of their native land of green and white, Hibernian, or Hibs as they're more commonly known, also adopted the Irish Harp as the club's official crest in homage to their Irish heritage. Inspired by the example of Hibernian were Dundee Harp, formed in 1879, likewise by Irish immigrants, though unlike their Edinburgh compatriots the Harp only enjoyed a brief existence before being disbanded in 1897 due to financial problems. As with Hibernian they played in green, as did another Irish Dundonian team, Dundee Hibernian, though for them it was green and black stripes.

Dundee Hibernian only lasted four years, however,

before they disappeared. But Dundee's Irish Catholic community would not be denied a football team of their own, despite the aforementioned failures, and in 1909 Dundee Hibernian were reborn, changing their name in 1923 to Dundee United. Along with the name change came a change in the club's colours, with white and black replacing green, then white only, until in the late Sixties finally settling on the distinctive burnt orange and black the club are associated with today.

As with Hibs, Dundee United sought to diminish their Irish heritage in later years and in this regard both have been successful.

In 1888 another Irish team was formed, this time in the East End of Glasgow, which rather than seek to downplay its heritage over its long history instead chose to continue to embrace it. The result has been a history that even the club's most passionate detractors would admit if being honest is deserving of the prefix great.

Celtic Football Club was the brainchild of Brother Walfrid (*above*), the religious name of Andrew Kerins, an Irish Marist Brother who'd arrived in Scotland the 1870s from Ballymote in County Sligo. A teacher by profession, Walfrid taught at various Catholic schools, and later founded St Joseph's Catholic College in Dumfries.

But notable though those achievements may be, Brother Walfrid's lasting legacy is the football club he formed in 1888 to raise funds to help the poor and destitute Irish Catholic immigrant population in the east end of Glasgow. The statue that stands pride of place outside Celtic Park today bears testimony to the values of solidarity and kinship that sustained his fellow countrymen and women at the end of the 19th Century, people whose lives were blighted by despair and the social maladies associated with crippling poverty in a land in which they were looked upon as little more than *untermenschen*.

But such a virulent strain of racism should not and cannot be viewed in isolation. For in the last analysis Scotland's Irish Catholic immigrant population were on the receiving end of the kind of treatment that colonisers and imperialist states have always meted out to those whose lands they wish to colonise and exploit.

In the year 1888 the British Empire under Queen Victoria was at its zenith in terms of size and dominion. It spanned a full three-fifths of the globe and controlled the lives and destinies of some 458 million people. In the words of its most famous chronicler and apologist, Rudyard Kipling, it was an empire so huge that upon it the sun never set - although my Irish grandfather Tommy Reilly always said that this was because God didn't trust the British in the dark.

Contrary to the literary efforts of Kipling and the other apologists for empire who came after him, the British Empire was not a force for good in the world, not the great civilising crusade unleashed by gentlemen to spread British Protestant values of jurisprudence, morality and democracy to heathen hordes.

Instead the British Empire was (and remains so under its modern incarnation as a loyal US gendarme scouring the globe looking for 'humanitarian' missions to unleash, usually involving oil rich nations in which British oil companies and corporations have significant investments to protect) forged to facilitate the systematic pillage and exploitation of natural and human resources on a mass scale, giving rise to the French novelist Balzac's famous dictum that, 'behind every great fortune lies a great crime.'

In Britain it was the age of private clubs, stately homes and huge unearned income from investments in colonial enterprises overseas, a genteel world of perfect gentlemen and fragrant ladies, members of a parasitic class dedicated to gorging themselves on luxury and pleasure, their priority keeping up the appearances, accoutrements and lifestyles expected of those accorded high social status.

Meanwhile, away from this rarefied world, the nation's slums were cesspits of despair, disease, crime and misery, depicted in scorching detail by the American novelist Jack London in his famous book, *The People of the Abyss*.

Here the great British Empire, that grand project to spread civilisation, order and Christian values throughout the world, devoured its own children in its giant factories and mills, where human beings were reduced to the status of those 'mere appendages of the machine' that Karl Marx described.

Despite inflicting so much despair and misery on so many both at home and abroad, monuments and statues were erected in every British town and city in tribute to the derring-do, enterprise and industry of those responsible. Military chiefs and generals, colonial administrators, political figures and others whose joint exploits in suppressing and exploiting millions by fire and sword should rightly have attached everlasting shame to their very names were instead lauded and celebrated.

The wealth expropriated from the colonies funded the grand edifices and the magnificent architecture that dominate British towns and cities today. In truth each and every one, every monument and statue, verily drips with the blood of the millions whose lives were rendered superfluous to the greed and venality of their colonial masters.

But trade and commerce boomed regardless, evident in the great ships that permanently clogged the ports of Glasgow, Liverpool and Cardiff, bringing with them the raw materials that went into producing the manufactured goods those same ships then transported all over the world.

Scotland, which unlike Ireland was not a victim of British colonialism but instead an eager participant and beneficiary, boomed. In Glasgow especially, home to a burgeoning merchant class, vast fortunes were made on the backs of the cotton, tobacco, and shipbuilding trades, with Glasgow soon earning itself the title of second city of the empire. Both the British Army and the British Colonial Office were liberally represented by Scots, who without exception set themselves to the task of maintaining order while exploiting the colonies overseas with enthusiasm and ruthless efficiency.

But Britain's colonies did not solely exist in far-flung lands in Asia, Africa and the Caribbean. By the late 19th Century Ireland had already existed under the iron heel of Britain's colonial might for over two centuries, first under the auspices of England and then later, after the 1707 Act of Union, Great Britain.

However, although obscured and even in some cases almost completely omitted from many of the official histories of British colonialism, the record shows that as with their fellow colonial victims around the world, the Irish refused to be enslaved and subjugated without a struggle.

The watershed moment in Ireland's anti-colonial history was the birth of the Irish Republican movement in 1791. Led by Wolfe Tone, a southern Irish

Protestant, it was a movement inspired by the republican ideals of the French Revolution and the belief in the universal and inalienable rights of all men to liberty and equality, as set out in Thomas Paine's famous work, *The Rights Of Man*.

It was Tone's desire to unite Ireland's 'men of no property', Catholic, Protestant and Dissenter (Christians who advocated no state interference in religious affairs), against the common oppression they shared at the hands of British landowners and the Anglican Church. This he did with the formation of the United Irishmen in 1791.

Catholicism had been proscribed in Ireland, and Ireland's native Protestants were increasingly discriminated against on the basis of their Irish ethnicity by the British. At its peak Tone's United Irishmen had over 200,000 members, a considerable number which back then constituted five per cent of Ireland's total population. Tone's plan was to coordinate an armed uprising with a French invasion of the country. In 1798 the attempt was made. However, largely due to lack of enthusiasm and limited participation by the French, it failed. In the process

Tone was captured.

From the dock at his trial, he made the following statement:

I have laboured to abolish the infernal spirit of religious persecution, by uniting the Catholics and [Protestant] Dissenters. To the former I owe more than ever can be repaid. The service I was so fortunate as to render them they rewarded munificently; but they did more: when the public cry was raised against me—when the friends of my youth swarmed off and left me alone—the Catholics did not desert me; they had the virtue even to sacrifice their own interests to a rigid principle of honour; they refused, though strongly urged, to disgrace a man who, whatever his conduct towards the Government might have been, had faithfully and conscientiously discharged his duty towards them; and in so doing, though it was in my own case, I will say they showed an instance of public virtue of which I know not whether there exists another example.

Tone died by his own hand while awaiting execution in Dublin. His lasting legacy is embodied in the following statement of his objectives:

To subvert the tyranny of our execrable government, to break the connection with England, the never failing source of all our political evils, and to assert the independence of my country--these were my objects. To unite the whole people of Ireland, to abolish the memory of all past dissensions, and to substitute the common name of Irishman, in the place of the denominations of Protestant, Catholic, and Dissenter.

Yet despite the fact that Theobald Wolfe Tone, an Irish Protestant, is today recognised as the father of Irish Republicanism, he and his United Irishmen were not the first Irishmen and women to resist their colonial overlords. In fact throughout the 17th Century, when the institution of slavery was still enshrined in English law and when Ireland had been an English colony for nigh on 400 years captured Irish rebels were sent to English slave colonies in the New World. Irish prisoners were sent to Amazonian settlements in 1612, for example, and an English Proclamation of 1625 urged banishment overseas of dangerous rogues (Irish political prisoners).

By 1650, during the reign of Cromwell, which saw terrible atrocities committed against the Irish people, the number of Irish condemned to slavery reached its peak, with estimates by historians lying somewhere between 80,000 and 130,000 men, women and children sent into bondage. Many were transported to the Americas to work the vast plantations in Virginia and New England. Most were sent to the Caribbean islands, especially Barbados, where thousands perished in the tropical heat from hunger and disease.

The British were proud of this policy, as can be noted in state papers published in London in 1742:

It was a measure beneficial to Ireland, which was thus relieved of a population which might trouble the planters. It was a benefit to the people removed, who might thus be made English and Christian, a great benefit to the West Indies sugar planters, who desired men and boys for their bondsmen, and the women and Irish girls to solace them.

Any Irish caught trying to escape were branded FT (Fugitive Traitor) on their forehead, whipped and/or hung by their hands and set on fire. And so that they might forget their religion, nationality and culture, most were given new names.

The Irish who flocked to the New World in the decades after the demise of Tone and his movement to end British rule in Ireland also demonstrated their solidarity with peoples struggling against oppression and colonialism. In August 1819 a thousand men of the Irish Legion landed on Venezuela's Margarita Island to fight in the armies of South America's Liberator, Simon Bolivar. More followed in the next few years, many of them earning high praise and great distinction from Bolivar for their dedication to his cause of liberating and uniting Latin America.

In 1846, thousands of Irish immigrants joined the

US Army and, under the command of General Zachary Taylor, were sent with his army to invade Mexico in a war of imperialist conquest and plunder.

Dubious about why they were fighting a poor Catholic country, and witnessing atrocities carried out on Mexican civilians by US forces, hundreds of them deserted Taylor's army and joined forces with Mexico. Led by Captain John Riley of County Galway, they called themselves the St Patrick's Battalion (in Spanish Los San Patricios).

They fought with bravery and distinction in most of the campaigns of the two-year conflict, but despite their efforts, and the bravery of the Mexican Army as a whole, the US onslaught proved too strong. After Mexico City came under occupation in 1848, Mexico surrendered, subsequently ceding nearly half its territory to the United States.

Towards the end of the conflict, at the Battle of Churubsco, 83 San Patricios were captured. Of the 72 who were tried for treason, 50 were sentenced to be hanged and 16 were flogged and had branded on their cheeks the letter D for deserter.

For obvious reasons the San Patricios were erased from the pages of US history for generations afterwards. However, in Mexico they have always been regarded as heroes. They are honoured to this day every September 12 with a special ceremony in Mexico City, where a commemoration pays tribute to their courage and heroism. In 1993 the Irish at last began their own ceremony of commemoration in Clifden, Galway, Riley's hometown.

While held prisoner in Mexico City Riley wrote to a friend back in the United States:

Be not deceived by a nation that is at war with Mexico, for a friendlier and more hospitable people than the Mexicans there exists not on the face of the earth.

The experience of the Irish Diaspora in the United States around the middle of the 19th century was not dissimilar to that of their Scottish compatriots. There, an anti-immigrant political doctrine known as Nativism gave rise to an organisation of native born, Protestant, white Americans who soon became known as the 'know nothings' on account of their policy of secrecy. As with Scotland's experience of anti-Irish Catholic immigrant movements the 'know nothings' were active on both a political level and in the streets, where they sought out and fought Irish gangs that had been formed out of the need for self-protection.

This period of US history, which merged with the rise of the movement for secession among the southern states and the onset of the US Civil War, was depicted in the Martin Scorcese film *Gangs of New York*, starring Liam Neeson and Daniel Day Lewis.

At the same time as Celtic FC was being formed in Glasgow, Ireland's struggle for justice was being led by another Irish Protestant in the shape of Charles Stewart Parnell.

However, unlike Tone and Robert Emmet (another Protestant Irish Republican who came just after Tone, and who likewise led an armed rebellion against the British that was crushed), Parnell took the path of reform by constitutional means, with the ultimate aim of Home Rule rather than complete independence through armed struggle.

Known as one of the best orators and statesmen ever to grace the British Parliament, Parnell was a complex figure – sympathetic to the ultra-nationalists of the Irish Republican Brotherhood on the one hand, while attached to the principles of constitutionality and the ability of the British Parliament to deliver meaningful reform on the other. What we do know is that he was able to convert the then Liberal British Prime Minister, William Gladstone, to the cause of Irish Home Rule, that he dealt a death blow to the long tradition of absentee landlordism in Ireland, and that he was the first Irish political leader to leverage the massive and increasingly influential Irish American community as a political factor in Ireland's cause.

On the other side of the equation, Parnell's success in pushing the cause for home rule in both Ireland and among the British political classes was met by equal determination on the part of Ireland's unionists, predominately located in the industrialised north of the country, to resist.

The sentiment among unionist leaders was that home rule would become 'Rome Rule', as they sought to exacerbate social division based on religion to ensure the continuation of the economic and social advantages that accrued to the North's Protestant industrialists and boss class. They feared that home rule would result in taxes being placed on their profits and property by a Dublin-based parliament and as a result were intent on bringing about its defeat by any and all means necessary.

In this they enjoyed significant support among Tories and unionist-supporting Liberals alike. In fact, the unionist-supporting Liberal faction ended up splitting to form the Liberal Unionist Party, before later joining with the Tories to form the Conservative and Unionist Party we know today. Here we see that Nick Clegg is merely the latest in a long line of those 'yellow Tories' who talk left and act right.

Perhaps the single most famous British political figure to align with the Ulster unionist cause was Lord Randolph Churchill, the father of Winston Churchill, who famously declared in 1886 at an Orange Order rally in Belfast that, 'Ulster will fight and Ulster will be right.'

The connection of the aforementioned political and social history with anti-Irish Catholic racism and bigotry in Scotland should be obvious. Events in

Ireland have always found an echo in Scotland's own political and social history, particularly in the west with its large Irish Catholic influence and heritage. The spread and influence of the Orange Order in Scotland which, as previously mentioned, was introduced into Scotland by Ulster Protestant immigrants in the mid to late 19th Century, helped to ensure that the assimilation of Irish Catholics into Scottish society was blocked, leading directly to the development by Irish Catholics of a separate community within a community - not out of aspiration but rather necessity.

In the way that Irish Catholics were viewed and treated in Britain and Scotland in particular in the late 19th and early 20th Centuries, we see similarities in the way that Muslims in this country are viewed and treated today. This is a topic I will return to later. Suffice to say for the moment that it is no coincidence that as someone who has dedicated his adult and political life to anti-racism and anti-racist causes I have been and remain active in confronting both.

But I digress.

The point is that it was as a result of this necessity to develop a network of mutual support and solidarity among Glasgow's Irish Catholics that Celtic Football Club was formed by Brother Walfrid in 1888.

Connolly, Billy Boys and Rangers

It is impossible to explore the history of anti Irish Catholic bigotry in Scotland, and the role of Celtic as a bulwark against it, without taking a look at the history and development of Rangers Football Club, Celtic's arch rivals and an institution long associated with the political and cultural aspirations of Scotland's, and the north of Ireland's, Protestant and loyalist communities.

Rangers were officially formed in 1873, although they actually played their first games the previous year in the form of two friendly fixtures against Callander FC and Clyde. They were formed by two brothers, Moses and Peter McNeil, along with Peter Campbell and William McBeath. There is no evidence that the club's Protestant and unionist identity was present at its formation or during the club's initial years but it is certain that by 1888, when Celtic were formed, the club enjoyed close ties with the Orange Order and had links with Freemasonery through its officials and directors.

By the early part of the 20th Century Catholic players at Rangers had been asked to leave the club, which from then on followed an unofficial policy of refusing to knowingly sign Catholics until 1989, when manager Graeme Souness signed Maurice 'Mo' Johnston.

By contrast, Celtic adopted an inclusive policy of signing players of every religious affiliation and creed from inception, a policy adopted after the club's officials and players held a vote on the issue. From then up to the present day Celtic has enjoyed an internationalist and anti-racist identity.

Twenty three years after Celtic were formed the 26-county Irish Free State was born as a result of the sacrifice and heroism of thousands of ordinary Irish men and women who succeeded in fighting the British state to a standstill. In the aftermath of the fighting, Collins and the rest of the Irish Treaty delegation to London were told in no uncertain terms by the British government of the day that the terms on offer – a 26-county Free State that would enjoy commonwealth dominion status, with the remaining industrialised and unionist dominated six counties in the North partitioned – were non-negotiable and that the alternative was total war and Ireland's destruction.

Collins reluctantly agreed to the terms put to him by the British on the basis that it was the best they could get and would at least constitute a stepping stone on the way to full independence for the whole of Ireland in the hopefully not too distant future.

In fact it wasn't to be until 1949 that the Free State withdrew from the British Commonwealth and formally declared itself a republic, while the six counties in the North continue to be partitioned.

But the real tragedy of the treaty with Britain that

was signed by the Collins-led Irish delegation and narrowly voted through the Dail was the brutal and ugly two-year civil war that followed. Families, friends and former comrades turned against one another as a result of the war which counts as one of the most tragic periods and events in Irish history, epitomised by the fact that Michael Collins, an Irish patriot, lost his life at the hands of fellow Irish patriots.

The catalyst for Ireland's War of Independence against the British state, indeed it could be argued the first strike in this war, was of course the 1916 Easter Rising in Dublin, when the Irish Volunteers, led by Patrick Pearse, joined forces with James Connolly's Irish Citizen Army to form the Irish Republican Army, before embarking on a brave but hopeless attempt to spark a nationwide rising with the aim of finally wrenching Ireland free from Britain's grasp.

James Connolly

In the aftermath of the Rising, which ended in inevitable defeat, 15 men, including the seven signatories of the famous Proclamation declaring Ireland's independence, were executed by the British. That their names would ring down through the years as symbols of patriotism and courage, taking their place in that illustrious pantheon of freedom fighters around the world who've sacrificed their lives and their liberty in the age-old struggle against oppression and colonialism, was thus guaranteed. A few days before being carried on a stretcher from his cell down to the courtyard of Dublin's Kilmainham Jail to face a firing squad James Connolly, in pain as a result of injuries he'd sustained during the fighting in the GPO in O'Connell Street in Dublin, had faced his executioners and said:

Believing that the British government has no right in Ireland, never had any right in Ireland, and never can have any right in Ireland, the presence, in any one generation of Irishmen, of even a respectable minority, ready to die to affirm that truth, makes the Government for ever a usurpation and a crime against human progress.

It should also be noted that Connolly had predicted that partition would lead to a carnival of reaction in the North. Even a cursory examination of the history of Partition proves that he was right.

But while those within the British military and political establishment in Ireland, who were responsible for deciding on the policy of courts-martial and executions, may have believed they were sending a message of deterrence, in truth they merely succeeded in spreading sympathy for a group of men who prior to the Rising had been widely perceived as cranks. Those same men had been on the receiving end of hostility from bystanders in the street as they were marched off to jail after they'd surrendered to the British.

The destruction of large parts of the centre of Dublin as a result of British shelling was deemed to be their fault. In addition the rebels were blamed for placing at risk the pension the Irish womenfolk received from the British government while their sons and husbands were fighting for the Empire in Belgium and France.

However this apathy and hostility soon turned first to sympathy then anger as one after the other the 15 were executed by a British military establishment in no mood to countenance clemency. The result was a renewal and increased support of a movement for Irish national liberation led by the likes of Collins and Eamon De Valera, which as mentioned resulted in the formation of the 26-county Free State five years later. To paraphrase WB Yeats in his famous poem commemorating 1916, a terrible beauty had been born.

The men who came after Connolly and Pearse and Plunkett were bolstered in their struggle by the all-Ireland elections to the Dail Eihreann (Irish Assembly) of 1919, also known as the First Dail, organised by Sinn Fein in defiance of the British in which Sinn Fein members enjoyed an overwhelming majority. It was a mandate for Irish independence by the people of Ireland that no amount of British repression could succeed in breaking.

But Ireland's struggle for independence cannot be

properly understood apart from the social and political upheaval sweeping through Europe at the same time, a direct consequence of the wholesale slaughter that was taking place in the trenches and which was to leave the national economies of the major European powers involved in tatters.

In 1917 the Bolsheviks in Russia, led by Lenin, took power after leading a successful revolution against the Tsar and the Russian nobility. Unsuccessful attempts to repeat the success of the Russian Revolution followed in Germany and Hungary, while in the Middle East the Ottoman Empire collapsed and the Arab world entered a period of European colonisation the effects of which remain to this day with the continuing injustice being inflicted on the Palestinian people.

Meanwhile in Scotland the era that came to be known as Red Clydeside saw thousands of workers in the country's industrial heartlands in and around Glasgow joining together to fight for better pay, the 40-hour week and an end to extortionate rents being charged by unscrupulous landlords, who'd taken advantage of the supposed vulnerability of wives and families whose men were away fighting in the war to fill their own coffers.

The movement culminated in a mass rally of 100,000 in Glasgow's George Square to commemorate May Day in 1919. Irish Catholics were prominent in the massive crowd, with Irish tricolours flying alongside the red flags which represented the workers' cause. Prominent Scottish radical and trade union figures such as John MacLean and Willie Gallagher shared the platform with Sinn Fein speakers. MacLean in particular was an admirer and supporter of the Irish struggle for independence, even producing a leaflet the following year titled *The Irish Tragedy: Scotland's disgrace,* on the role of Scottish soldiers in committing atrocities in Ireland during the War of Independence.

Around the same period the Orange Order formed the Patriotic Workers League, an organisation of strike-breakers, in a naked attempt to characterise the mass strikes that were taking place as the work of Fenians and other foreign aliens. But for this brief period working class consciousness was able to break through the usual attachment on the part of the Protestant and unionist working class to king, empire and country, with the example of the Russian Revolution a major contributing factor.

However this lessening of anti-Irish Catholic racism and bigotry merely constituted an all too brief departure from the norm. Throughout the interwar years, despite the increasing influence of the Labour party in Scotland, which had opened its doors to Scotland's Irish Catholic community, Catholics were typically blocked from taking up skilled employment by a combination of bigotry among employers and Protestant skilled workers and their trade union leaders alike, among whom Orangeism and Freemasonery exerted a huge influence.

By the mid-1920s the manifold benefits of the British Empire to Glasgow's fortunes were gradually being overtaken by a rise in poverty, depredation and their social consequences as the Great Depression approached.

One of those social consequences was the growing size and preponderance of gangs, with easily the most notorious of these the anti-Irish Catholic Billy Boys, formed in 1924 by Billy Fullerton after he was involved in a physical confrontation with Catholic youths on Glasgow Green.

Fullerton was an early example of the ideological connection that has always existed between loyalism and fascism, and indeed in the late 1930s Fullerton joined Oswald Mosley's British Union of Fascists. Based in and around Bridgeton Cross in the East End of Glasgow Fullerton and his gang eagerly sought confrontation with Catholics by staging Orange walks through Catholic areas of the east end.

There they came up against Irish Catholic gangs, in particular the Norman Conks, and the street battles that ensued are now part of the city's social history, handed down from generation to generation despite the efforts of succeeding generations of the city's hierarchy to expunge it.

Glasgow's reputation as one of the most violent cities anywhere in the industrialised world began during this period, with Billy Fullerton (*below*) and his Billy Boys a major factor in establishing it. As the famous novel put it Glasgow was No Mean City – but for many it was all too mean!

During the 1920s Fullerton and his gang also proved an able and willing tool in the hands of the bosses and right-wing Tory politicians who employed them as strike-breakers and to break up socialist and trade union meetings during the 1926 General Strike. In return for services rendered Fullerton and leading members of his gang were awarded medals and various other tributes from said bosses and right-wing politicians.

To this day the memory of Billy Fullerton and the Billy Boys is kept alive in the stands of Ibrox and every other stadium Rangers visit by the song which bears his name and celebrates the anti-Irish Catholic bigotry he championed both in word and deed.

Hello, hello, we are the Billy Boys
Hello, hello, you'll know us by our noise
We're up to our knees in Fenian blood
Surrender or you'll die
For we are the Brigton Billy Boys.

How many good working class supporters of Rangers who find themselves signing this paean of praise to Fullerton know they are singing in support of the bosses' bully boys and later fascists?

Protestant reaction

The rise of fascism and race-based politics in Europe in the 1930s found a willing home in Scotland as a result of the country's culture and history of anti-Irish Catholic bigotry and racism.

In Scotland it manifested in the growth in popularity of the Scottish Protestant League led by Alexander Ratcliffe. Formed in 1920, it was 10 years later that the league began to make inroads as a political force at local level when in 1931 Ratcliffe was elected onto Glasgow City Council, one of two seats the organisation won that year.

The following year the Protestant League contested 11 wards in Glasgow and gained a third seat, winning 12 per cent of the total vote. In 1933, the year of Hitler's ascension to power in Germany, the Protestant League stood in 23 Glasgow municipal wards and managed to secure 71,000 votes, riding the wave of anti-Catholic and anti-immigrant sentiment that was prevalent during the Depression.

The main plank of the league's platform was the repeal of the (1918) Education Act, in particular the section which provided for the entrance of Catholic schools into the state system funded through local rates. The League coined the slogan *'No Rome on the Rate'* as part of their campaign to have the act repealed.

Ratcliffe and the Protestant League were also committed to stopping Irish immigration to Britain, repatriating those Irish immigrants who were already settled in the country, and deporting any Irish immigrants who were on welfare.

But lest anyone think that Ratcliffe's Protestant extremism can be easily dismissed as marginal, the ideas he promoted gained traction at the highest levels of the British establishment. In fact, under pressure from the Orange influence that obtained in the country at the time, Ramsay McDonald's National Coalition government gave consideration to those same anti-Irish immigrant proposals in 1933. The Orange influence within the government was illustrated by the presence of two Scottish Orangemen in his cabinet: the Home Secretary, Sir John Gilmour, and the Scottish Secretary, Sir Godfrey Collins.

Much like the British National Party of today the Protestant League combined racist policies with progressive ones calling for more council houses and reducing rents and rates for those people who they'd deemed ethnically and religiously fit to live in Scotland.

As to its founder and leader Alexander Ratcliffe, a fascist in all but name hitherto, he officially became one after a visit to Germany in 1939, the same year that Britain entered the war and sent her young men to resist the Nazi menace.

On Wednesday May 11, 2011, at Tynecastle Park in Edinburgh, during a Hearts v Celtic league match, Celtic manager Neil Lennon was attacked by a fan who had managed to get on to the pitch. The incident shocked and brought shame not only to Hearts and to Scottish football, but also to the nation in general, coming as it did in the wake of five intercepted mail bombs to prominent Irish Catholics and individuals associated with Celtic Football Club, one of whom was also Neil Lennon.

For many in Scotland the fact that this kind of sectarian attack could take place in the nation's capital came as a shock, exploding the myth that anti-Irish Catholic bigotry was an exclusively West of Scotland phenomenon.

The incident at Tynecastle Park came as no surprise to me. Nor would it have come as a surprise to anyone with even the briefest experience of attending football matches at Tynecastle over the years, which to the initiated isn't known as Little Ibrox for nothing.

In fact the sectarian chanting that takes place on a regular basis at Tynecastle is second only to that which takes place at the home of Rangers. I myself have spent some of the most unpleasant afternoons and evenings of my life sitting in the stands at Tynecastle. It is there that I have found myself in a state of fear and alarm at the sustained gratuitous sectarian chanting accompanied by threats of violence and much more than in any other place.

I have been in Beirut under bombardment, in Gaza under siege, in Eritrea being bombed by Ethiopian government jets dropping American-supplied bombs, have lived in Glasgow during the Orange marching season, but I have never been more afraid or felt more at risk at any other football match than in Scotland's capital city. And over many years.

One deeply unpleasant individual who has a minor part in this story later on is the laughingly entitled Lord George Foulkes. He is a former chairman of Hearts FC and his son was convicted following a Hearts game at Tynecastle for what the Lothian and Borders police described as the longest, most sustained episode of sectarian abuse they had ever seen.

Lord George - a Labour member of the Scottish Parliament and who sat with me in the House of Commons for many years - has long been a political enemy of mine. But even I had to feel a little bit sorry for him after an incident which ties us together, forever

I was coming up the escalator from the underground car park of the House of Commons when passing me on the down escalator was the then Lord Hughes, formerly Bob Hughes, Member of Parliament for Aberdeen North, a left-wing MP sponsored by the engineering union and a champion of the anti-apartheid movement

As we met momentarily halfway up the escalator, or down in his case, he told me to look at that day's Daily Telegraph because he was sure I had a libel action in the making - not for the first and certainly not for the last time.

'What's it about?' I asked his lordship as he disappeared.

I made for the Commons famous library where I probably spent literally years of my life and immediately looked for the Daily Telegraph. There sure enough was the offending article.

The report stated that George Galloway MP had two nights previously staggered drunk out of a reception held by the Scotch Whisky Association in Westminster, knocked over two old ladies, assaulted a policeman manhandling his bobby's helmet, slept it all off in a cell in Charing Cross police station, appeared in court the next morning, was heavily fined, smuggled back into parliament on the floor of colleagues shooting brake, carpeted by the late Labour leader John Smith and dismissed from the Labour front bench.

As you will have gathered there were several problems with this article. First as a teetotaller I have never tasted whisky, never attended a soiree of the Scotch Whisky Association, never knocked over two old ladies, never handled a bobby's helmet, never spent the night in a police cell, not been convicted nor fined, never smuggled into parliament on the floor of a car, never carpeted by the late John Smith, never sacked from the Labour frontbench on which I'd never sat. Apart from that it was scrupulously accurate!

You'll know by now, of course, that the criminal in

question was none other than the former chairman of Hearts FC. He commented after the attack on Neil Lennon that perhaps the answer was that Celtic should play in the Irish league!

But anti-Catholicism and Edinburgh enjoy a wider political as well as a cultural and sporting connection. For around the same time that Alexander Ratcliffe and his Protestant League were making waves in Glasgow a man by the name of John Cormack (*left*) was doing the same in Edinburgh with his Protestant Action movement, which had similar success in local and municipal elections and were also not averse to taking their message out into the streets with regular incursions into Catholic areas of the city, mostly in Leith.

By the mid 1930s Protestant Action had pushed Labour into third place in Edinburgh with Cormack enjoying increasing popularity with his anti-Catholic, No Popery tirades from the soap box. That said, Cormack was noted for his opposition to a visit by Oswald Mosley to Edinburgh in 1934. But this was based on Mosley's support for a united Ireland and Mussolini's ties to the Vatican rather than any commitment to anti-fascism.

Ratcliffe and Cormack both saw their political fortunes go into decline as a result of the Second World War, which given the reactionary and fascistic brand of Protestant extremism that both men upheld was no surprise or coincidence.

The decade immediately after the war saw the Scottish and British working class more united than at any other time in its history. This was the result of the introduction of the welfare state by the post-war Labour government and the advent of full employment, which mitigated competition for jobs among the working class, Protestant and Catholic alike. It was a period of renewal, prosperity and hope, as the world entered a new era of progressive politics after the dark years of fascism and the barbarism it had inflicted on its millions of victims.

Meanwhile, Celtic also entered a new era after the disruption of the war years when Jimmy McGrory (*above*) took charge of the team in 1945. His outstanding achievements as a player were alas not matched by his achievements as a manager, with Celtic winning few honours in the post-war decade. They did win the Coronation Cup in 1953 however, a one-off tournament to commemorate the coronation of Queen Elizabeth II, defeating Arsenal, Man United, and the great Famous Five Hibs team on the way to lifting the trophy.

The Fifties under McGrory were also notable for the record 7-1 victory over Rangers in the 1957 Scottish League Cup Final, a result that still stands to this day as a record in a British domestic final. Billy McPhail scored a hat-trick after Sammy Wilson and Neilly Mochan, the first Celtic player I ever met, had put Celtic 2–0 up at the break. Mochan added to his tally in the second half and Willie Fernie rounded things off with a penalty towards the final whistle.

As the club entered the Fifties, however, Celtic's toughest opposition lay off the pitch, when the club found itself under attack in the face of determined campaign led by the Scottish Football Association to remove the Irish tricolour from the ground, where it had flown proudly since the club was formed and where it still flies proudly to this day in tribute to the club's Irish heritage. No matter, all of a sudden the SFA and its supporters were adamant that the flag had no place in Scottish football and were determined it be removed on pain of Celtic being expelled from the league.

The leading light in the SFA's anti-tricolour campaign was its secretary George Graham, later knighted for his services to football. It is also significant that Harry Swan, the chairman of Hibernian FC, was a key figure, illustrating the extent to which the Edinburgh club had turned away from its own Irish heritage. Fortunately the campaign failed to succeed - though only by a single vote, which ironically came from Rangers.

Before this is held up as evidence of the Ibrox club's departure from its sectarian reputation the Rangers vote was more to do with ensuring that their own policy of refusing to sign Catholics did not itself come under scrutiny as a quid pro quo if the tricolour was banned from Celtic Park.

Here again we see the attempt to draw an equivalence between a club's national heritage, in the case of Celtic, and another club's religious sectarianism, in the case of Rangers.

So far throughout this book, repeated references have been made to the Orange Order and its role in helping to establish and sustain a culture of anti-Irish Catholic bigotry in Scotland. Perhaps then it is worth taking a moment to explore the organisation's history and philosophy.

On its official Scottish website the Orange Order describes itself as, 'the oldest and biggest Protestant fraternity in Scotland,' going on to state that, 'We are an organisation of people bonded together to promote the great ideals of Protestantism and Liberty.'

Here, in only the first two sentences of the Order's mission statement, we find a blatant historical untruth. For the fact is the Orange Order both in Northern Ireland and Scotland was founded in the 18th Century precisely to help crush the cause of liberty - in particular to resist the advance of the emancipatory ideals of the French Revolution which in Ireland were embodied in the struggle waged by Wolfe Tone and the United Irishmen to unite the 'men of no property', both Catholic and Protestant, against the oppressive rule of the landlords and monarchism.

Moving to the history section of the Grand Orange Lodge of Scotland's website we are met with the following half way down the page:

In spite of this disunity both branches of the Order continued to grow, in part due to the ever increasing flow of Ulstermen into Scotland who boosted the numbers in existing Lodges and formed new ones, but also as native Scots reacted to the growing number of Roman Catholics competing for jobs in the industrial centres, and as Catholics were granted more and more concessions by successive Liberal Governments.

Placing to one side for the moment the fact that the argument promoted in this section – that Roman Catholics constitute an alien and threatening presence – contradicts the section of the lodge's own mission statement which boasts, '*The Protestant ethic is one of tolerance of other faiths and ideals. It is this tolerance and liberty that the Orange Order promotes and defend*'. This openly supports an ideology of religious and racial supremacy that would not be out of place in the literature of the Ku Klux Klan in the United States.

Further on in the same history section we encounter the following:

The Loyal Orange Institution of Scotland therefore entered the new century with a particular optimism, although a series of miners' strikes and economic recessions caused membership levels to fall off a little.

The reason why membership of the lodge 'fell off a little' was precisely because of the its role in upholding the interests of the bosses and its long and sustained political attachment to the forces of reactionary conservatism in Britain. In other words the class interests of the rich as opposed to the working class to which most to the rank-and-file of the Orange Lodge actually belong - if only they would admit it and accept it.

The Orange Lodge in Scotland was particularly active in opposing the (1918) Education Act, which provided for the state funding of Catholic schools in Britain. The argument against the act put forward by the lodge at the time was that it enshrined religious apartheid. It is the same argument we've heard being rolled out recently as a rationale behind the continuing cancer of anti-Catholic bigotry.

This is of course preposterous, especially as a separate Catholic education system also exists throughout Europe and in the United States, state-funded and supported, without it being upheld as a cause of social division or strife.

The simple truth is that Catholic schools are a symptom of religious persecution and bigotry in Britain, not its cause. Moreover, Britain is not a secular country. How can it be when an unelected monarch is both head of state and also the head of the officially established Protestant church? Therefore it is entirely reasonable and correct that Roman Catholics are afforded the right to protect their own religious traditions and educate their children in an environment that upholds that tradition.

To deny them this right in favour of an education system that is dominated by a Protestant Christian ethos would be tantamount to turning Catholics into second class citizens. It is for this reason that I believe that Muslims and other significant religious minorities should also be granted this right, thus embracing the values of multiculturalism rather than the monoculturalism that some, including those secular fundamentalists who inhabit much of the left, advocate.

Today, though the Order is nowhere near as big or influential as it was in days gone by, there are still over 900 Orange Lodges in Scotland with an estimated total membership of around 50,000. Each year there are literally hundreds of Orange Walks throughout the British Isles, with the bulk of those taking place in Scotland, mostly around the 12th of July in commemoration of the Battle of the Boyne in 1690.

Orange Walks are commonly, though not always, integrated with wider loyalist marches, making them indistinguishable from their avowedly more extremist anti-Catholic counterparts. In fact loyalist marches and Orange walks are nothing more than aggressive triumphalism and naked displays of triumphalism and anti-Catholicism, wherein militarism and violence are celebrated. As such they have no place in a civilised society and their banning is long overdue. The fact that they still take place is testimony to the cowardice of the nation's politicians at both local and national level in their accommodation to bigotry and racism.

Unsurprisingly, Rangers Football Club is an institution with long historical links to the Orange Order in Scotland. As previously mentioned, strong links between the club and the order were evident by the early part of the 20th Century when Rangers adopted an avowedly Protestant identity and the policy of refusing to sign Catholics was instituted.

Since that time many of the club's directors,

officials and players have been Orangemen, and lest anyone think that this connection has diminished with time the unveiling of the all-orange Rangers away kit in the early Noughties, unconvincingly portrayed as a tribute to the Dutch manager and several players, should give them cause to think again.

Be realistic, demand the impossible

Britain's social history is replete with the continuous arrival of new waves of immigrants, predominately from nations of the former Empire and Commonwealth to meet the demands of the bosses and beneficiaries of the nation's economy for cheap, flexible labour as the indigenous population moves up the economic and social ladder to occupy the skilled jobs and professions that are off-limits to those freshly arrived immigrants for at least a generation, when they are finally assimilated and more or less accepted as part of the nation's social fabric.

Throughout the 19th and early part of the 20th Centuries it was predominately Irish immigrants who arrived in the country. From the end of the Second World War all through the Fifties Afro-Caribbeans arrived in their thousands from the West Indies and Jamaica to take up menial employment as cleaners, hospital porters, and factory girls. The same with the Asians who began arriving from India and Pakistan in the Sixties and Seventies, although as a result of the strong tribal, religious, family and community ties that are an intrinsic part of their culture they soon established themselves as small businessmen and women, opening up newsagents and grocers as well as establishing the chains of fantastic restaurants most of us enjoy today.

Chinese immigrants have also added to the nation's cultural mix to help create the diversity that has been a never-ending source of strength and benefit to British society. Today, in any town and city throughout the land, you have a choice of cuisine from every part of the world, every music, art form and cultural tradition, and you will be enriched by the experience.

When I compare this to how it was in a city like Dundee in the Sixties and early Seventies when a night out consisted of sausage and chips, egg and chips or mince pie and chips, followed by a night in the pub listening to Billy Fury, I cannot conceive how anyone could possibly pine for the lost, monochrome identity of pre-immigration Britain.

Yet anti-immigrant politics have been adopted by the mainstream parties in recent years, including the party to which I devoted 36 years of my political lifesblood – the Labour party. This isn't so much motivated by political principle as an opportunistic attempt to dredge support among a parts of the white working class whose primary source of news and ideas come from an increasingly reactionary and poisonous tabloid culture.

The owner of most of these gutter newspapers in Britain is Rupert Murdoch, a right-wing billionaire who pays hardly a penny of income tax in this country, who isn't even eligible to vote yet who through his press and broadcast news empire wields a distorting and malign influence over the nation's political process and whose hirelings are being increasingly exposed as lawbreakers and common criminals.

Murdoch is a serial patriot having started life as an Australian made his pile in Britain before becoming a patriotic American worshipping the greenback rather than the outback and certainly giving no payback to the British working class who filled his pockets. Now with a Chinese wife perhaps Rupert Murdoch will have time to squeeze in one last spasm of fake patriotism as he follows his rising star in the east.

The easiest and most politically expedient thing in the world in times of economic recession for the typically spineless coterie of entrenched and smug careerist politicians who fill the benches of our parliament - along which I often saw a shiver looking for a spine to run up! - or when it's time to unleash another war for oil and corporate profits overseas, is to distract people's attention with dog whistle attacks on asylum seekers, immigrants and as is increasingly the case, Muslims.

Today in Britain Muslims are regarded much the same way as Irish Catholics were a hundred years ago in Scotland – a scorned and disdained minority whose culture and religion is deemed inferior, regressive and a threat to the purity of the dominant culture and the perceived privileges of its adherents.

Yet as a result of the close ties between Ireland and Scotland and the long struggle in Ireland between unionism and republicanism this anti-Irish Catholic racism and bigotry of a hundred years ago remains embedded in large sections of Scottish society. This was never more so than during the Troubles that afflicted the six counties for over 30 years.

But again, as with previous periods of turmoil in Irish history Ireland in the late Sixties, when the Troubles erupted, cannot be viewed in isolation from world events, which is why it is crucial we take a look at the wave of radicalism, protest and anti-colonialism that shook the world throughout a decade that was and continues to be synonymous with progressive politics and social change.

The civil rights movement in the United States, specifically in the South where blacks suffered racism, intimidation and state sanctioned apartheid, actually began in the mid-1950s.

Its seminal moment and catalyst came when Rosa Parks got on a public bus in Montgomery, Alabama and refused to give up her seat at the front for a white passenger. Parks was arrested and convicted of disorderly conduct by the local authorities. But in so doing they only succeeded in lighting the touch paper of a movement that would sweep not only across the entire southern states but the whole of the United States and then the world, courtesy of television.

The Montgomery bus boycott that followed Rosa Parks' arrest and conviction succeeded in desegregating the town's municipal bus service, in the process proving how effective a campaign of civil disobedience could be.

A key figure in the Montgomery bus boycott campaign was a young Baptist minister by the name of Martin Luther King. Hitherto unknown, suddenly King found himself being catapulted via the new mass medium of television into homes all across America and the world, including by the mid-Sixties a tiny corner of northern Europe where there were people also being deprived of their civil rights, this time not on account of the colour of their skin but their religion.

However, it wasn't just in the United States where young people were rising up against injustice, repression and colonialism. In Paris, London, Rome, Berlin mass movements sprang up during the same period, while in Vietnam the Vietnamese were resisting the might of the US military in a war to liberate their country from western colonialism and imperialism.

TV footage and pictures of this seemingly rag-tag army of pyjama-clad men and women taking on the might of US imperialism and winning, driven by the desire to free their country from its long history of foreign occupation and colonialism, first at the hands of the Japanese, then the French and now the Americans, inspired anti-colonial movements throughout the developing world, in the process destroying forever the racist myth that non-white people were incapable of standing up, to never mind defeating, their white colonial masters.

In tandem with events in Vietnam the Cuban

Revolution was continuing to cast its spell over young people the world over with its iconic and charismatic leaders Fidel Castro and Che Guevera. Alongside all this in the west a cultural revolution in music and fashion and the arts was underway, again driven by a new generation of young people from the ranks of the working class who wanted and demanded more out of life than their parents had before them and who were determined to be heard and shape a world in which human beings were the end and not just the means to the end.

It all seems very naïve and unrealistic today but then as one of the main slogans of the French student and worker uprising of 1968 put it: 'Be realistic, demand the impossible.'

Each movement fed and inspired the other, creating for a brief period a world in the grip of resistance to the established order in which the possibility of meaningful social and political change seemed within reach.

The non-violent mass movement that began in the southern states of America lit the spark of its Irish counterpart which began in the late-Sixties under the auspices of the Northern Ireland Civil Rights Association (NICRA).

One of its leaders, John Hume, with whom I sat

in parliament for many years, would go on to help found and later lead the SDLP. He was only too happy to credit the US civil rights movement with inspiring the movement he joined and played a key role in as a young student.

'The civil rights movement in the United States was about the same thing, about equality of treatment for all sections of the people, and that is precisely what our movement was about,' said Hume when looking back at these events in the years that followed.

NICRA's objective was equal rights for Catholics in the North. That was it. Nothing about a united Ireland or an end to British rule. Just equal rights with the Protestant and unionist majority in a part of the UK where Catholics were denied equal access employment and housing, electoral representation due to the lack of housing rights (at the time only registered tenants were eligible to vote in local elections in the North, and with Catholics denied housing by a unionist-controlled local government, this meant they were denied a vote) and where they were subjected to regular intimidation and violence by a sectarian militia that had the temerity to describe itself as a police force. The specific demands of the movement were as follows:

+ one man, one vote - specifically the extension of the local government franchise from ratepayers to all those over 21
+ an end to gerrymandering (the drawing of

electoral wards to ensure unionist majorities in elections even in areas where Catholics and nationalists were the majority community)
+ an end to discrimination in housing
+ an end to discrimination in jobs
+ the disbandment of the B-Specials, the sectarian police auxiliary

As with its US counterparts the mostly young men and women, both Catholic and Protestant and predominately students, who comprised NICRA's leadership implemented a campaign of sit-ins, marches, pickets and non-violent protest to pressure the Northern Ireland government into granting their demands.

Adopting the anthem of the black civil rights movement, the black gospel hymn *We Shall Overcome*, they thus further drew the connection between two peoples who may have been divided by an ocean and ethnicity but were bound together by those bonds of common humanity and suffering that throughout history have always transcended divisions of geography, race, religion and culture - and always will.

The other attribute that both movements held in common was the huge courage of those involved, young men and women willing to expose themselves to physical harm each time they took to the streets to confront the hatred, racism and bigotry of the status quo. Who could ever forget the news footage of black protesters being clubbed by racist police officers in Mississippi and Birmingham, of having vicious dogs set on them, of being on the receiving end of water cannon, all in the name of preserving a system of apartheid and the material and imagined privileges attached to that system?

In the north of Ireland similar images of protesters being clubbed and beaten by bigoted thugs in uniform were flashed across the world, embarrassing a supine British government and shining a light on the sectarianism and bigotry that was being allowed to pass for democracy under its jurisdiction.

The names of some of those involved in NICRA have become familiar, people such as Ivan Cooper, Bernadette Devlin McAliskey, and as already mentioned, John Hume.

McAliskey (*left*), who remains to this day active in the cause of social justice, summed up the spirit and determination of those involved when she famously stated that, 'To gain what is worth having, it may be necessary to lose everything else.'

Those were not mere empty words where she was concerned as along with her husband McAliskey was shot during an assassination attempt in 1981 after loyalist paramilitaries forced their way into her home.

Such was her devotion to the struggle for social justice regardless of where it was being waged in the world that in the early 1970s, when awarded the keys of New York by the city's Irish-American mayor John Lindsay in tribute to her work as a champion of Catholic civil rights in Northern Ireland, McAliskey gave it to the local chapter of the Black Panther Party, who themselves were involved in a struggle for social and economic justice in the US. As she explained it:

'I was not very long there [America] until, like water, I found my own level. 'My people' — the people who know about oppression, discrimination, prejudice, poverty and the frustration and despair that they produce — were not Irish Americans. They were black, Puerto Rican, Chicano. And those who were supposed to be 'my people', the Irish Americans who know about English misrule and the Famine and supported the civil-rights movement at home, and knew that Partition and England were the cause of the problem, looked and sounded to me like Orangemen. They said exactly the same things about blacks that the loyalists said about us at home. In New York, I was given the key to the city by the mayor, an honour not to be sneezed at. I gave it to the Black Panthers.'

Even as an elected MP to the British parliament, where she sat from 1969-1974 McAliskey made her presence felt. In the wake of the atrocity of Bloody Sunday in 1972 when 14 protesters were shot dead by soldiers of the Parachute Regiment during a civil rights demonstration in Derry Bernadette McAliskey punched the then Conservative Home Secretary Reginald Maudling, after he made a statement in the Commons declaring that the Paras had acted in self-defence. McAliskey earned herself a suspension from the Commons for her actions, but of far greater significance was the respect and admiration she received from her own people and people all over the world for her stance against oppression and injustice.

It was the great Polish revolutionary, Rosa Luxemburg, who said that, 'Those who do not move do not notice their chains'.

And like her Bernadette Devlin McAliskey's life has been dedicated to breaking not only her own chains and those of her people, but the chains of oppressed people everywhere?

Bloody Sunday was an act of mass murder that effectively brought to a violent and tragic end the non-violent Northern Ireland Civil Rights movement. The fact that succeeding British governments until relatively recently refused to acknowledge the event as an act of murder only added insult to injury for the families of the bereaved and their communities.

But while the peaceful civil rights movement may have ended, the oppression that gave rise to it hadn't. As such, resistance now took the form of armed struggle and with it the emergence of the Provisional IRA as first defenders of Catholic and nationalist communities which were under attack from loyalist gangs while the authorities looked on, and then as the latest incarnation of a long tradition in Ireland of physical force republicanism committed to ending British rule.

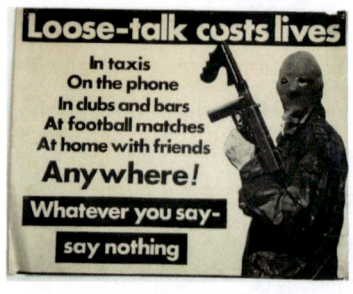

The words of John F Kennedy had proved eerily prescient in this regard: 'Those who make peaceful revolution impossible will make violent revolution inevitable'.

Celebrating Irish roots

I am a strong supporter of Sinn Fein and the peace process in the Six Counties. In fact, I was a supporter of Gerry Adams back when he was still considered persona non grata in this country and as I discuss elsewhere I still bear the scars to prove it.

I always sensed that he was a man struggling to move Irish Republicanism onto the political terrain where it belongs and I believe that history will accord him and Martin McGuiness their rightful place as men of courage and vision for having done so.

The Troubles were a tragic period in Irish and British history alike, during which both the best and worst of humanity was in evidence at various points. The toll taken in human life, the emotional and psychological scars inflicted, and the hatred and mistrust entrenched as a consequence will remain a festering sore in the North for years to come.

However, any proper analysis of the Troubles must begin with an understanding of the social injustice that gave rise to them, injustice that I have already explored.

I did not of course support all of the republican movement's' tactics, indeed some I condemned at the time and still do now. I believe they made errors of judgement which deepened and compounded sectarian division within the North. But I understand completely the serious political objectives which motivated Irish republicanism, objectives that I fully supported then and continue to support.

One thing I certainly do acknowledge was the courage and self-sacrifice of the republican hunger strikers in the Maze Prison, the infamous H-Blocks, 10 of whom chose death in protest at the ending of the status of republican inmates as political prisoners by the British government.

Led and inspired by Bobby Sands (*left*), they proved beyond doubt that theirs was a political struggle, this despite the massive propaganda campaign to the contrary that had been unleashed by Thatcher's government through its allies and supporters in the mainstream press and media to the effect that Sands and his comrades were common criminals. No common criminal could die with the courage of Sands and the other hunger strikers.

Though it may be easy to forget now through the prism of time the global impact of the Irish hunger strikes was immense. Upon the death of Sands in 1981 a letter paying tribute to him and the struggle for which he gave his life was smuggled out by Palestinian prisoners being held by the Israelis as a result of their own struggle. It reads as follows:

To the families of the martyrs oppressed by the British ruling class. To the families of Bobby Sands and his martyred comrades.

We, revolutionaries of the Palestinian people who are under the terrorist rule of Zionism, write you this letter from the desert prison of Nafha. We extend our salutes and solidarity with you in the confrontation against the oppressive terrorist rule enforced upon the Irish people by the British ruling elite.

We salute the heroic struggle of Bobby Sands and his comrades, for they have sacrificed the most valuable possession of any human being. They gave their lives for freedom.

From here in Nafha prison where savage snakes and desert sands penetrate our cells, from here under the yoke of Zionist occupation, we stand alongside you. From behind our cell bars, we support you, your people and your revolutionaries who have chosen to confront death.

Since the Zionist occupation, our people have been living under the worst conditions. Our militants who have chosen the road of liberty and chosen to defend our land, people and dignity, have been suffering for many years. In the prisons we are confronting Zionist oppression and their systematic application of torture. Sunlight does not enter our cell; basic necessities are not provided. Yet we confront the Zionist hangmen, the enemies of life.

Many of our militant comrades have been martyred under torture by the fascists allowing them to bleed to death. Others have been martyred because Israeli prison administrators do not provide needed medical care.

The noble and just hunger strike is not in vain. In our struggle against the occupation of our homeland, for freedom from the new Nazis, it stands as a clear symbol of the historical challenge against the terrorists. Our people in Palestine and in the Zionist prisons are struggling as your people are struggling against the British monopolies, and we will both continue until victory.

On behalf of the prisoners of Nafha, we support your struggle and cause of freedom against English domination, against Zionism and against fascism in the world.

Meanwhile, Cuban leader Fidel Castro made the following statement at the opening of a speech he gave in Havana.

In speaking of international politics, we cannot ignore what is happening in Northern Ireland. I feel it is my duty to refer to this problem. In my opinion, Irish patriots are writing one of the most heroic chapters in human history.

They have earned the respect and admiration of the world, and likewise they deserve its support. Ten of them have already died in the most moving gesture of sacrifice, selflessness and courage one could ever imagine.

Humanity should feel ashamed that this terrible crime is being committed before its very eyes. These young fighters do not ask for independence or make impossible demands to put an end to their strike.

They ask only for something as simple as the recognition of what they actually are: political prisoners...The stubbornness, intransigence, cruelty and insensitivity of the British government before the international community concerning the problem of the Irish patriots and their hunger strike until death remind us of Torquemada and the atrocities committed by the Inquisition during the apogee of the Middle Ages. Most tyrants tremble before men who are capable of dying for their ideals, after 60 days on hunger strike!...It is high time for the world community to put an end to this repulsive atrocity through denunciation and pressure.

Elsewhere, in the Indian parliament of the day opposition members stood and observed a minute's silence in tribute to Sands, while the Iranian president sent a message of condolence to his family. In addition the Iranian government of the day renamed Winston Churchill Boulevard in Tehran, where the British

Embassy was located, Bobby Sands Street, prompting the embassy to move its entrance door to avoid having to print Bobby Sands Street on its letterhead.

Incidentally, I once visited the British Embassy in the capital of then a revolutionary Mozambique. On the British government's letterhead, resplendent, was the embassy's new address: Vladimir Ilyich Lenin Boulevard!

In Europe a protest in solidarity with Sands and the other hunger strikers in Milan saw thousands of students turn out, during which they burned the Union Jack. In Paris another demonstration was staged, during which the marchers held pictures of Sands and his comrades as they chanted tributes to the men. In towns and cities throughout France there are streets named after Bobby Sands as a result of the hunger strike.

There was a similar response to the death of Bobby Sands in Scandinavia and throughout north America. In fact, all over the world his death was met by an outpouring of tributes, protests, and messages of condolence, solidarity and support.

By now you may be asking what any of this has got to do with Scotland. As I've already stated, political events in Ireland, especially the North after partition, have always had an impact in Scotland, particularly in the west of the country, as a result of the deep association forged between both countries due to mass Irish immigration to Scotland on the one hand and the negative and bigoted reaction to it on the other.

In Scotland the Troubles gave rise to songs in praise of the IRA at Celtic Park and at every ground where Celtic played. Likewise at Ibrox songs lauding the exploits of the UDA and other loyalist paramilitary organisations now became a regular occurrence. Whilst fully understanding how and why such songs are offensive to many there is still no equivalence between songs that promote racism and bigotry based on race or religion and songs which support an organisation or doctrine that is political in orientation.

You see Irish Republicanism is not and never has been a doctrine rooted in religious sectarianism or racism and any such attempt to draw such a connection must be resisted. Attempts to conflate songs in praise of Irish republicanism – like *The Boys Of The Old Brigade*, which celebrates the struggle for independence – and the campaign against British rule with sectarian racism or bigotry are simply wrong.

Songs such as *The Fields Of Athenry* or *A Soldier's Song* are neither sectarian nor racist. The former is an Irish folk ballad while the latter is the national anthem of the Irish Republic. Both fall into the category of celebrating Celtic and its supporters' Irish heritage and both are therefore entirely legitimate.

Over the years countless football writers, commentators and officials have lamented the merging of football with politics in Scotland, castigating the fans of both Celtic and Rangers for sectarian songs and propagating the sectarian divide that exists in the country at large.

Here again we see evidence of either deep-seated ignorance or a wilful misrepresentation of the facts surrounding this issue. There is no sectarian divide. There is on the contrary a history of anti-Roman Catholic bigotry, with a particular emphasis on Roman Catholics of Irish persuasion or heritage, which remains embedded in a significant section of Scottish society and culture.

But there is no moral equivalence between the *Famine Song* and *The Fields of Athenry*. One is clearly racist, while the other is not.

The Souness revolution

In 1986 Graeme Souness was appointed player-manager of Rangers. It was an inspired appointment by the club's board, chaired at the time by David Holmes. Holmes worked for the new Rangers owner David Murray as a director of his company and was parachuted in to transform the moribund club. And from the start he made it clear he would sweep away all the old anathemas – or what some supporters would call traditions.

Souness is a man impossible not to admire, a class act both on and off the pitch who was an integral part of the great Liverpool side of the late Seventies and early Eighties, before going on to play at the highest level abroad with Sampdoria in Serie A. He also enjoyed an international career that saw him grace the stage of three World Cups for his country.

Souness arrived at Ibrox at a period when Scottish football was in the doldrums, post the great Ferguson and McLean eras at Aberdeen and Dundee United respectively. The Old Firm had fallen on hard times relative to former days, with both clubs regularly making zero impact in Europe, resulting in their fans increasingly being forced to cast a nostalgic eye back to the glory days of yore for comfort.

Celtic were in particularly dire straits, hampered by a board whose ability to run the club lay somewhere between unimaginative and inept. Rangers at least had had the foresight and ambition to redevelop their stadium while it would take Celtic another decade to finally revamp theirs, and this after an acrimonious battle to change the ownership of the club. Here I must pay tribute to my good friend Brian Dempsey, who was instrumental in saving the club from financial disaster during this period. And I wish him a speedy return to the top.

When Souness arrived at Ibrox he immediately unleashed what came to be known as the Souness Revolution which swept Scottish football. For the first time in the history of the game north of the border the migration of top Scottish talent to England was put in reverse, with the signing of the likes of Terry Butcher, Chris Woods, Graham Roberts, Mark Walters, and Mark Hateley, and other England internationals by the club over the next few years. At the time English clubs were banned from Europe because of the Heysel Stadium disaster when rioting at the start of the 1985 European Cup Final between Liverpool and Juventus left 39 Juve fans dead and 600 injured.

By far the most important and significant signing that Souness made during his reign at Ibrox was Maurice 'Mo' Johnston in 1989, the first high-profile Catholic to ever sign for the club. The fact that Souness managed to prise Johnston away from Celtic who, under Billy McNeill, had thought that they'd secured his services just days prior, only added to the huge controversy surrounding the move, one that made international news.

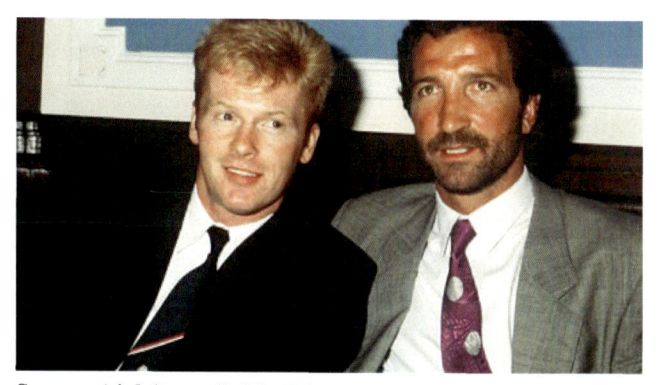

Souness (right) unveils Mo Johnston

Almost 20 years later Souness would say: 'Every manager politically would say yes (about signing a Catholic) but I actually meant it. I was married to a Catholic, my children were christened Catholics. I was brought up in Edinburgh. Every day I walked with a Catholic friend to school. It was never an issue in our house. I was brought up by very level-headed, right-thinking parents. Maybe I was naive but religion just wasn't an issue to me.'

It was the shattering of a long and seemingly unbreakable taboo where Rangers were concerned and in hindsight it could only have been broken by a man of Souness's stature. The reaction of Rangers fans to the signing of Johnston was one of shock, bewilderment and from many a sense of betrayal. Many vowed never to attend Ibrox again and some even burned their scarves and season tickets. The general secretary of the Rangers Supporters Association at the time, David Miller, said, 'It is a sad day for Rangers. I don't want to see a Roman Catholic at Ibrox'.

Remember as you consider that quote that it was given in Scotland in 1989 and not 1889.

Celtic fans were no less angry at Johnston signing for Rangers. However, unlike Rangers supporters such as David Miller, their anger wasn't motivated by bigotry but by a deep-seated sense of betrayal.

Off the park Johnston never went anywhere without a bodyguard, while on it you'd never guess he was affected by any of the aggro surrounding him as he proceeded to slot into the Rangers side and quickly win over the Ibrox faithful with an appetite for goals that helped the club on its way to its nine in a row league titles, matching the record previously set by Celtic.

But if things had changed on the park under Souness, off the park and in the stands anti-Irish Catholic bigotry remained ever present. *Up to our knees in Fenian blood* remained the ubiquitous refrain at places like Ibrox and Tynecastle Park, and in the case of Rangers even the takeover of the club by David Murray in 1988 failed to produce any real change in this regard. In fact, if anything, the culture at Rangers post-Souness grew even worse and more poisonous, with first team players such as Paul 'Gazza' Gascoigne and Andy Goram embracing the loyalist image of the club with various gestures and antics both on and off the park.

Gazza excuse may be that he's merely a simple idiot. That he mimicked playing the flute on the field in a Rangers game because he didn't realise the significance. I doubt it. I had my own exposure to Gazza's mimickry. I was in the British Airways lounge in Glasgow waiting on a flight one Saturday evening when Gascoigne burst in and downed several glasses of free champagne in rapid succession. When he got on the London flight he alternated between drinking more alcohol and whistling the Sash while playing an imaginary flute in the front row of the plane.

Perhaps most illustrative of the culture within the club at the time was the video of Rangers director, Donald Findlay QC, singing the Sash at private party organised by the Rangers Supporters Club to celebrate Rangers' victory over Celtic in that season's Scottish Cup Final. Findlay was forced to resign from the club's board, but clearly there was no sense of shame at his debacle for in 2005 he was taped making anti-Catholic jokes at another Rangers Supporters event, this time in Larne in the north of Ireland.

The fact that Findlay happened to be a high-profile figure within the Scottish legal establishment at the time, and indeed still is, as evidenced in his 2010 election as chair of the Faculty of Advocates Criminal Bar Association, will not be lost I'm sure on anyone reading this.

In 1995 a young man by the name of Mark Scott had his throat sliced open while walking through Bridgeton Cross one Saturday afternoon. The reason for his murder was that he had on a Celtic shirt under his top. He'd just been to a match at Celtic Park and was on his way home, choosing to make his way in the direction of the centre of Glasgow along London Road through the notoriously loyalist supporting Bridgeton Cross area of the east end, formerly the heartland of the Billy Boys. If he had taken the safe route along the Gallowgate he would still be alive today.

He was killed for no other reason than he'd chosen to demonstrate his support for a football club and a sporting institution that is associated with Glasgow and Scotland's Irish Catholic community. His murder inspired the creation of the anti-sectarian charity, Nil By Mouth, which to this day continues to campaign for an end to sectarianism in football.

Meanwhile, the defence of the man who was tried and convicted of Mark Scott's murder, Jason Campbell, an avowed loyalist whose father was a leading member of the UVF, was conducted by none other than Donald Findlay QC.

Before the trial began I was visited by Strathclyde Special Branch officers who told me that my name, Glasgow address and contact details had been found in Campbell's belongings.

Sadly, this brutal sectarian murder of young Mark

Scott was mirrored in February of this year, 2011, when 18-year-old Raemonn Gormley was killed in High Blantyre as he was walking home from watching a Celtic match on television.

Reid all about it

One of the most shameful events in Celtic's history as far as I'm concerned was the appointment of Dr John Reid – or to give him his proper title, Lord Reid of Cardowan – as the club's chairman in 2007. **Along with the many around the world I consider John Reid to be a war criminal, with the blood of untold hundreds of thousands of Iraqi men, women and children on his hands.** I believe that Brother Walfrid could be heard spinning in his grave upon the appointment of this man as Celtic chairman, an appointment indicative of political and moral degeneration of an institution that throughout its history has always stood for something more than success on the pitch or commercial advantage off it.

I have a long history and long experience of Dr Death which began as long ago as the 1970s when he was a hardline member of the pro-Moscow Communist Party of Great Britain. He was a supporter of Irish republicanism, too, teaching many of us the republican songbook.

When I was the youngest ever chairman of the Labour Party in Scotland at the age of 26 Dr John Reid was my research officer and whilst I always admired his skill and knowledge it came as no surprise to me when after the defeat of Michael Foot in the 1983 general election that Reid, together with Gordon Brown and a small group of others, began to hijack the Labour party we had and fly it to destruction.

In its place Reid and Co constructed a mutation. Labour became New Labour, became Non-Labour ending up as Anti-Labour, airbrushing its history, ideology, purpose and even former leaders as efficiently as any KGB rewriting of history.

Reid moved to London to work in the House of Commons for Neil Kinnock the apostate who began the destruction of Labour as we knew it, before regretting it. I moved to London in 1983 very soon after he did. Our paths frequently crossed and cross we were at what each other was saying and doing.

At the time John Reid had a serious drink problem, indeed the late John Smith QC – one of the leaders airbrushed by the group that came to be led by the war criminal Tony Blair – warned him that if he did not give up drink Smith would give up on him. To his great credit John Reid kicked his drinking habit but not before two incidents of note.

The first is when John Reid fought the SAS…well, a former member of the SAS to be precise. Few people know that the attendants in the inner sanctum of the House of Commons are almost all former members of Britain's elite Special Air Service.

The British Parliament continues to employ the most absurd method of legislators casting their votes of any in the world. Instead of the pushing of an electronic button or the insertion of a card or the use of a barcode in the British Parliament each member – there was 650 when I was there – must physically crush into a voting lobby which is a small and narrow hall in which it is physically difficult for everyone who wishes to vote to fit.

Moreover from the moment that the Speaker of the House of Commons calls the vote this 650 members must make a dash for this lobby from wherever they are on the Parliamentary estate or nearby and they have just eight minutes to get both feet inside that lobby.

At precisely eight minutes after the Speaker has called the vote he will shout – 'lock the doors' – and the powerfully-built attendants do precisely that. If you're on the wrong side of that door when it locks your vote is null and void.

One night John Reid and I were dashing for the same vote and he was one person in front of me in the queue. When the speaker cried 'lock the doors' John Reid had one foot in the lobby and the other not. The ex-SAS man gave Reid a hearty push in the chest to get him out of his way. Now where John Reid and I come from we don't take kindly to people pushing us even if they are wearing uniforms and formerly served in the SAS. In fact, particularly so.

So Reid pushed back and buoyed up no doubt with Dutch courage shaped up and challenged the doorman. Within a second the self-styled hard man of Blair's government lay more or less unconscious at my feet, a position he has never attained since.

Another was in 1991 during the first Anglo-American war against Iraq. Reid had been the deputy spokesman for Labour in parliament on children. With war raging Neil Kinnock had brought out the worst in him by unleashing what turned out to be a latent talent for war propaganda. One afternoon after he and I had clashed in the chamber of the House of Commons Reid walked, well staggered really, from the chamber into the voting lobby with me hot on his heels: 'You bastard,' I said, 'you have gone from an Irish republican communist to a mouthpiece for American imperialism. You've gone from spokesman on children to apologist for the murder of children. You make me sick.'

Reid lurched towards me his fists raised to shape up. Now I am a non-drinker, and a good few years younger than him, and I used to be a boxer. So far from being afraid I relished what was about to happen. I hit him with straight right to his solar plexus and a left which skidded off his right ear. But just as the knockout uppercut was leaving my right shoulder he was literally saved by big Diane Abbott, then as now the redoubtable – and anti-war – Labour MP for Hackney who launched herself on top of him knowing that I would never hit a woman – indeed never hit anyone as powerful as Diane.

I continue to love her to this day but I can never

forgive her for denying me that uppercut!

It's not just that Lord Reid defiled everything he ever believed in, destroyed with his friends the short-term possibilities of achieving what he used to believe in for the rest of us. It's not just that he was a mouthpiece for every murderous war which came afterwards.

It's not just that he was the Secretary of State for Northern Ireland, most beloved by Ulster loyalists. It's not just that he helped privatise Britain's public services or that he was viciously hardline Home Secretary, a cross between a hanging judge, J Edgar Hoover, a tinpot Churchill desperate for a siege of Sydney Street to attend. It's not just because he scraped the barrel of anti-immigrant prejudice in pursuit of racist votes.

It's all of the above and much more!

His departure as chairman of Celtic, announced just as I was putting the finishing touches to this book, is surely a welcome development.

But no matter who the chairman of either Celtic or Rangers may be the fierce rivalry between the clubs and the hatred that exists between the supporters is a reflection of a social division that has long and deep roots within Scottish society. The clubs merely reflect and provide the forum where this division is most commonly and publicly expressed and are not its cause. Rangers, whether they like it or not, and despite the various anti-sectarian initiatives the club has facilitated over recent years, are associated through their fans and the club's history of anti-Catholicism with a racist and reactionary creed known as loyalism, which as I've explored in this book has strong links to fascism, militarism and colonialism.

Is it any surprise that frequently at Rangers matches you will see the Israeli flag being flown, while at Celtic there can often be seen Palestinian flags? One represents the triumphalism of a settler colonial state and the apartheid and racist system it has given rise to, while the other represents resistance to that apartheid and racism.

It is also no accident that along the Falls Road you will find murals paying tribute to the Palestinian struggle for freedom and justice, linking it with the Irish struggle for the same. This is why the Irish tricolour has the same connotation as the Palestinian flag in my view – both symbols of resistance to colonialism and the racism and apartheid it has spawned.

Having said that, the Queen's historic state visit to the Irish Republic in May of 2011, where she laid a wreath in the Garden of Remembrance in Dublin in tribute to those who fought and died to liberate Ireland from British rule, before going on to visit Croke Park, scene of the first Bloody Sunday massacre in 1920 when British troops entered the stadium during a Gaelic football match and fired into the crowd indiscriminately, has to be considered a spectacular success. Though no fan of the monarchy, any monarchy for that matter, personally I thought Queen Lizzie played a blinder.

The problem of course remains the small matter of partition, the bastard child of colonialism the world over, whether in Kashmir, Ireland, or Palestine. Unionists in the North of course have the right to wish to remain part of the United Kingdom, and judging by the desultory protests that took place in Dublin against the Queen's state visit, the people of the South are not exactly clambering to reclaim the Six Counties for Ireland either. However, partition is not only an issue of sovereignty. It is also, and perhaps even more importantly, an issue of separation within the partitioned state. Because despite the huge progress made as a result of the peace process in bringing an end to the armed struggle, it hasn't succeeded as yet in bridging the religious and social divide that remains as much a part of life in the north of Ireland today as it ever has.

Time and continued political engagement will hopefully combine to solve this particular conundrum. Regrettably, being the student of colonial history that I am, I feel bound to say that I have my doubts. Partition has always and everywhere been the cause of division and hatred in the world.

Born in a bad time

Neil Lennon was born in Lurgan on June 25 1971, in the first years of what become known as the Troubles in Northern Ireland, and just weeks before internment was introduced.

He was the second child of Gerry and Ursula Lennon, and named after the nickname of his maternal grandfather, Neilie. So Neil it was and not, fortunately for him, his grandfather's given name, Cornelius. Lennon has said that the abiding sound of his childhood was of whistles blowing, metal clashing and women wailing. The sound of death.

Like many town in Northern Ireland Lurgan was demarcated along religious and political beliefs, Catholic and republican and Protestant and unionist. One of Lennon's earliest memories of the house in Edward Street, in the middle of Lurgan was the long line of concrete barrels and metal piping in the road between his house and his grandfather's, there to stop car bombs being placed.

'We were constantly being evacuated from the house because of bomb scares,' he said 'which were usually, but not always, hoaxes. One Friday,' he continued, the day when his mother made his favourite stew, his sister Orla was carrying the pot from the oven to the dinner table when a massive explosion shook the house. Orla dropped the pot and burst out crying. 'I was more upset that she had spilled the stew all over the floor...'

In 1976 the Lennons moved to a new house on the Taghnevan estate on the edge of the town. Growing up the family avoided the direct tragedies which marked so many other families but in October 1990 one of his schoolmates Dennis Carville was murdered.

He happened to be a Catholic, in the wrong place at the wrong time. Dennis and his girlfriend were in his car at a nature reserve, Oxford Island on the south end of Lough Neagh. It was a well-known lovers' spot. There was knock on the window from what appeared to be a soldier. He was in fact a member of a Loyalist paramilitary group. He asked for Dennis's driving licence, established he was a Catholic and shot him in the head from inches away .

'It could have been any of us Catholic boys from Lurgan,' recalled Lennon, 'who got the bullet that killed Dennis.'

Dennis was 19 as was Neil Lennon, then living on the mainland in Stockport. Lennon has never hidden his beliefs from the world. He was raised a Catholic, baptised in St Peter's Church in Lurgan and made his first Holy Communion and received confirmation in St Paul's church, which served Taghnevan. Taghnevan was an all-Catholic, Republican estate, along the lines of the religious apartheid which cut the country into enclaves. Lennon describes it:

> *The worst period for tension and violence was undoubtedly the time of the hunger strikes in the early 1980s. The country was on the edge of all-out civil war during that long campaign by the Republican prisoners, led by Bobby Sands who, despite being in prison, had been elected an MP shortly before he died from the effects of self-starvation.*
>
> *You could always tell when a hunger striker had died.*
>
> *As soon as news of the death broke, no matter whether it was in the dead of night or during the day, people would come out of the houses and would start to bang metal bin lids, either thrashing two together or thumping them off the pavement. Whistles would be blown at the highest possible volume, and men and women would shout the news. The noise would spread through the estate and sometimes there would be women wailing and frightened children screaming.*
>
> *I was only nine or ten at the time, but I can remember that cacophony as if it was yesterday. On one occasion a hunger striker died and the noise of the bin lids and the shouts or protest reverberated around the estate in an unearthly*

> *manner. It was as if the banshee of ancient Irish folklore had suddenly come to life in Lurgan. I was truly frightened as I lay in bed.*
> (Neil Lennon, Man and Bhoy. HarperSport 2006)

Lennon has vivid memories of many of the major event of the Troubles, like the murder of Airey Neave in the House of Commons, the bombs which killed Earl Mountbatten and those which killed the 18 British soldiers on a bank holiday at Warrenpoint, just down the road from Lurgan. He admits that before he moved to England as a professional footballer he did sometimes get caught up in the street rituals of the nationalist youth at the time, chucking stones at the soldiers and the police, the Peelers, then almost exclusively Protestant.

But football was the life and Neil's overwhelming interest. He says he is in awe of the people and the sacrifices they made so that he and his friends could play football. 'Getting us kit and a place to play, transporting us all over the country and beyond, coaching us, keeping us safe and arranging for some us to be looked at by senior team, and all this against a background of the Troubles. Neil joined Lurgan Celtic Boys' Club at the age of 10. His career had begun.

'For as long as I can remember my team was Celtic. My Dad supported them. Most of the rest of the family were fans and they were very important to us and to many people in our community as shown by the fact that one of the biggest clubs in the town was Lurgan Celtic....I dreamed of one day playing for them.'

The first time he saw Celtic in the flesh was at a friendly in Dundalk and then a second time with his boys' club to watch them play in the Scottish cup semi-final of 1983 against Aberdeen, managed by Alex Ferguson. They lost 1-0.

'It was one of the few times in my life that I saw my father look absolutely stunned.' A letter from Rangers arrived out of the blue inviting him over for a day. Rangers were then, and had been for more than a century, exclusively Protestant. He travelled to Ibrox and was shown around by Jimmy Nichol, the Northern Ireland international. Unsurprisingly the interest came to nothing.

But after playing a couple of games for Irish League side Glenavon in 1987 Lennon was signed by Manchester City, although that portion of his career was ruined by a back injury which required major surgery and extensive rehabilitation. That explains his subsequent, stiff, upright running gait.

From City he signed for Dario Gradi's Crewe Alexander. Gradi preaches passing football, keeping the ball on the ground and Lennon loved it. After five years and 181 appearances Lennon signed for Leicester City and Martin O'Neill, another mentor who would play a hugely influential role in his professional life.

O'Neill recalls first meeting Lennon on a beautiful summer's morning not far from Lurgan. O'Neill was on the first rung of the managerial ladder, with Wycombe Wanderers, Lennon was trying to rebuild his life after the injury, with Crewe. Years later, again as O'Neill recounts it, and now manager of Leicester, he drove with his assistant John Robertson to a 'rundown hovel' in Stockport to try to persuade the occupant to help him get promotion with Leicester rather than sign for Premiership club Coventry.

The witnesses to the meeting were, apparently, a couple of mice in the corner inured to the early Oasis music bleeding other ears.

Clearly O'Neill's plaintiff appeal defeated the blasts from the Man City-supporting Gallagher brothers and Lennon gave his word he would sign for Leicester. After three-and-a-half seasons with Leicester Lennon followed O'Neill to Celtic.

The rest is this history.

Crimes and misdemeanours

Neil Lennon would be the first to admit that he has tangled with controversy over the years. He has never been on to pull out of a tackle, either on or off the field.

On of the most memorable – although it was one which might well have occasioned amnesia – was in April 1998 when he was playing for Leicester at home against a struggling Newcastle side, then sixth from the bottom of the league.

It was the 57th minute, Lennon was going for a ball near the touchline, trying to shield it when the Newcastle and England captain Alan Shearer grabbed him, they both fell to the ground, and Shearer kicked Lennon viciously in the head. Blood spurted from his nose, and a cut above his eye. The referee, Martin Bodenham, gave a foul against Lennon for the initial challenge and took no action against Shearer. As he lay there dazed Newcastle's David Batty ran over and tried to pull him off the pitch.

Martin O'Neill was incandescent: 'I do not care whether you are Alan Shearer or the Pope, you just do not do that. I saw Lennon get kicked in the face. Of course it was deliberate. He should have got sent off.'

The incident made headlines throughout the world and after a barrage from the media the Football

Association belatedly called an inquiry. Newcastle were FA Cup finalists and if found guilty then Shearer would certainly be banned. Gary Lineker, ironically a former Leicester player, Glenn Hoddle, the England manager and other English football worthies, came out to say Shearer hadn't meant it – even the late Tony Banks MP, then the Minister of Sport, defended Shearer. Lennon, approached by the head of the PFA, Gordon Taylor, appealed to, and then phoned by a worried Shearer, decided to speak on his assailant's behalf.

The FA's three-man panel ruled that, 'The alleged incident of Alan Shearer swinging out with his left leg was a genuine attempt to free himself.'

Not according to Lennon. 'It was the World Cup year and all those people came out – Gary Lineker. Glenn Hoddle. The fucking sports minister – all to say Shearer hadn't meant it. I'm thinking, "Did I headbutt his fucking boot or something?" But it's not a good idea to get kicked by the England captain.'

The telephone call which was to change Lennon's life wasn't even made to him. It was late afternoon on August 21 2002, when an anonymous caller phoned the BBC's office at Ormeau Avenue in Belfast. He didn't say his name but left enough hints as to his background. His message was brief and to the point:

'This is the LVF [Loyalist Volunteer Force]. If Neil Lennon takes the field tonight he will get seriously hurt.'

'It didn't matter to the caller that I had lived away from Northern Ireland for 14 years,' Lennon recalls. 'He didn't know that my family was not associated in any way with political or sectarian groups. It only mattered that, for the first time, a Roman Catholic who also played for Celtic would captain Northern Ireland against Cyprus in Belfast.'

The seeds of what happened that night were laid on the evening of February 28 2001. That was the first time he had played for Northern Ireland after joining Celtic, in a friendly against Norway at Windsor Park.

Neil's last appearance for Northern Ireland

Lennon was expecting stick. 'But nothing could have prepared me for the sheer scale of what happened before and during that match.'

A few days before the game, 'Neil Lennon RIP' had been scrawled on a wall near his parents home. His Gerry had not been well and was to suffer a heart attack in August 2001. He, and Neil's mother Ursula and the rest of his family, were deeply upset by what some moron undoubtedly thought was a sick joke.

Worse, much worse, did come his way.

From the moment he went on to that pitch to play against Norway he was the target of an unremitting chorus of boos, jeers, catcalls and insults. In a half-empty stadium, the noise seemed to amplify and at times it seemed as though it was the only sound to be heard. There was a small crowd at the game, around 7,000, and the minority might only have been 500 or 600, but to Lennon 'the proportion booing me didn't matter - one per cent would have been too much'.

Lennon was used be being booed and was almost blasé about the anti-Catholic songs sung at Windsor Park internationals before but, like most Catholic players, like Martin O'Neill before him, played on. This was different. 'This was something else again and was, I believe, completely premeditated,' said Lennon. 'I had played 35 times for my country before that night and had a good relationship with most fans, who knew I gave my all for Northern Ireland. So what had happened to make things so different? Answer: I now played for Celtic'

Martin O'Neill had been the first Catholic to captain Northern Ireland. He and Lennon had even talked about this kind of possibility when he was persuading the Neil to follow him to Celtic. But neither O'Neill nor Lennon could have anticipated this.

'There is a difference of opinion about what took Opinions differ as to what took place at half-time, but Lennon's recollection is that Sammy McIlroy (the Northern Ireland manager) said him that he had spoken to Martin O'Neill about taking him off at the interval before the game in any case. Given that Neil was relatively new at Celtic and shouldn't be playing every minute of every game, it sounded plausible.

However, Martin O'Neill has no memory of such a conversation. Lennon speculates that McIlroy might have said this at the time to cover up the deep embarrassment which he and the Irish Football Association's officials were feeling. Lennon believes that this was simply cowardice.

Neither McIlroy nor anyone from the Irish FA confronted the issue at the time and there were no warnings to the crowd that Lennon heard. So the bigoted minority got their way. 'The football pitch can be a very lonely place,' Lennon said later, 'and I never felt so isolated in a match as I did that night.'

Lennon played two World Cup qualifiers against Bulgaria, missed three games but was picked for matches running up to the European Championships.

On his 41st appearance for his country against Cyprus he was appointed captain..

As he has said: 'I was honoured, and my family were proud and delighted for me. At a press conference I emphasised that the events of the Norway game were in the past and that I preferred to look forward. I said honestly that it had been difficult at the time, but I had put it all behind me. The political situation in Northern Ireland had also changed. It was now more than four years on from the Good Friday Agreement, and I thought there was genuine goodwill on all sides. But one man in a phone box many miles away thought differently.'

At the pre-match meal when Sammy McIlroy took him aside. Two police officers from the newly-named Police Service of Northern Ireland were outside wanting to talk to him. There been a phone cal, he said, but Lennon would have to talk to the officers about it.

He instinctively knew what the call was and his heart sank into his boots. 'In the run-up to the match I knew I was "fair game" for any madman wanting to make a point and I had anticipated someone trying to get publicity for their "cause", especially after it was announced that I would captain the side. But I had not thought it would go as far as someone threatening my life.'

There had been a telephone threat to the BBC's offices in Belfast by someone who claimed to represent the LVF. The threat was that if he played that night he would get hurt. Without it being needed to be said, he knew that in all probability hurt meant getting shot.

Lennon asked the officers if they thought it was a genuine threat. They replied that nine out of 10 of these calls were hoaxes. They were firm, however, that they could not tell him what to do. That decision would have to be his. He took that to mean an escort to and from the game. But how would they prevent someone getting to him in one of the public areas of Windsor Park?

At first he decided he would play. Then a maelstrom of thoughts pulsed through his head – thoughts about his family and their safety – but finally it came down to a wager. How much of a bet do you take with your life?

He decided to withdraw.

Sammy McIlroy reacted well and sympathetically. He said that if the call had been about his son, he would want him to go home.

Neil called his parents. His father said that of course he shouldn't play and he would come and get him. They had had a police escort at first but then some friends met up with the car and they travelled in convoy for the rest of the journey.

Lennon has never been back to Windsor Park since and his Dad still has his unused tickets for the match in which Neil Lennon did not captain Northern Ireland.

The incident became headline news and Lennon even considered quitting Celtic and football entirely.

As he put it, 'No one except another footballer can really know about the long hard hours of work that go into reaching the top level that is international football. All the other sacrifices such as special diets and the rigours of self-discipline all count towards your achievements, and here was I with the pinnacle of my career to date snatched away by a man with a telephone.'

One English journalist wrote he was a 'big girl's blouse' for not risking death., although he did not have the courage to say it to his face. What must have been the most upsetting speculation was that pulling out of the game served some sort of hidden agenda on Lennon's part. As Lennon said in his autobiography, Man and Bhoy, 'It's the sort of biased reasoning which has seen me burned in effigy on the tops of bonfires across Northern Ireland on July 12, the great Unionist and Protestant day of celebration - I must be rivaling Guy Fawkes for being "toasted".'

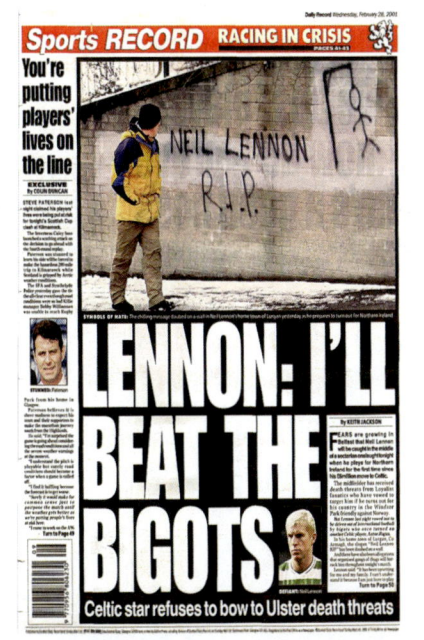

Trouble in Paradise and beyond

I suppose it's only people of a certain age who remember Harold Wilson, the Labour prime minister who led two administrations in the 1960s and 1970s. When I met him at his home he was in the terminal stages of Alzheimer's. He could recall every word of a speech he had made in Huddersfield in 1955, but couldn't remember anything from a few minutes ago. As a result I had to tell him, what seemed like a thousand times, that, no, I didn't really want another slice of cake.

Wilson, who had been one of the best, the brightest, and certainly youngest-ever Cabinet minister of the 20th Century at 31, was noted for his aphorisms and flowery speech, and one of them has gone into the annals of political quotes. 'A week is a long time in politics,' – as true then as now.

I was reminded of it in the embarrassment over the new bill on anti-sectarianism, which was meant to be passed before the start of the football season, and ended up by being kicked into the long grass, at least for the time being. The First Minister, Alex Salmond, had told the country that the new bill would be a massive leap forward in the drive against religious hatred at football matches. Seven days later he was forced into an embarrassing climbdown.

'We will not tolerate sectarianism, as a parasite in

our national game of football or anywhere else in this society,' he said on May 18. The Offensive Behaviour at Football and Threatening Communications (Scotland) Bill, published on June 17, proposed two new offences, each punishable by up to five years in prison and an unlimited fine. First, offensive behaviour at football matches, covering sectarian, racist, or homophobic abuse. Second, threatening communications, including emails, blog posts, and Twitter messages, which could lead to violence or 'religious hatred'.

The government said the bill had to be fast-tracked through Parliament in a fortnight to be in place by the start of the football season on July 23. While that meant limited time for scrutiny, "immediate action" was needed to respond "quickly and decisively".

But almost immediately, it was clear that other political parties, church groups and lawyers were unhappy about such a significant proposal being dropped on them without any warning. Craig Whyte, the new owner of Rangers FC, waded into the debate, denying the club had a problem with sectarian singing at Ibrox (despite it being fined £35,000 for that just a few months earlier), and warned Salmond not to single out his side in the crackdown on bigotry. The game was up when Celtic went public and said the act would be unworkable.

The Community Safety Minister Roseanna Cunningham's appearance before Holyrood's justice committee effectively killed the present incarnation of the bill. Despite insisting speed was vital, she admitted she'd had little time herself to read some early comments on it. Asked if singing the national anthem or Flower Of Scotland might be an offence, she initially said no, then dug herself into a hole by saying it depended on circumstances, adding that even making the sign of the cross could be "aggressive".

The next day's headlines screamed that singing Rule Britannia or blessing yourself now meant jail. The Scottish Police Federation also said ministers were "way off the mark" on the costs of enforcing the new laws. My old pal Ian Smart, past-president of the Law Society of Scotland, said: "It's a terribly drafted piece of legislation. I think the government desperately grabbed at things to put into it. It's difficult to see anything that's not already illegal."

Conservative justice spokesman John Lamont also took the debate in an uncomfortable direction for ministers by criticising the education system as a crucible of sectarianism. Lamont said dividing children between Catholic and non-denominational schools was "state-sponsored conditioning of sectarian attitudes".

On June 24, a week later, Salmond announced that the fast-tracked bill would now be withdrawn, temporarily at least. There'd be a six-month hiatus before it came back.

Salmond is nothing if not a consummate political realist.

Called to account

Immediately after the attack on Neil Lennon I posted a blog on Facebook about it, which produced hundreds of responses – the overwhelming number of them positive and approving.

Dying of shame: The bigotry which dare not speak its name

by George Galloway MP on Thursday, May 12, 2011 at 9:10am

Forget that rather facile comment by a legendary manager about football being more important than life or death, to a present-day one it is about just that. Or rather more specifically, death.

Neil Lennon, the manager of Celtic, is a Catholic, a republican and courageously outspoken. It shouldn't be necessary to append these adjectives to his name but it is because of them that he has received his latest live death threat, a bullet in the post.

Prior to that there have been deadly letter bombs and more bullets, his home in Glasgow's West End is bristling with security devices, his wife has to go to a safe house with their child when Celtic are travelling and Lennon is under police protection, but clearly of the most cursory nature. On Wednesday evening as he stood on the touchline guiding his team to victory over Hearts at Tynecastle a home supporter leaped the wall scampered past what is laughably known as security and landed a blow before being overpowered by Lennon's coaching assistants. His assailant hasn't appeared in court yet but you couldn't get odds anywhere that the man is anything other than a virulent and violent Protestant bigot.

If Neil Lennon decides at the end of this week and the league campaign that he's chucking it in then no one would blame him. Scotland, however, would die of shame.

The reaction in Scotland has been curiously muted. It's as if that because we've lived with anti-Catholic bigotry for so long it's not unexpected, if slightly over the top. Some have even turned it onto the victims, that it's really the Tims' fault for maintaining separate schools. If those letter-bombers or that attacker had just shared a sandwich with a Catholic at play times if would never have come to this.

Some even went further. George Foulkes, Baron Foulkes of Cumnock, is a former chairman of Hearts, the club the attacker follows. He's a lickspittle Labour man with a despicable record. In 1993, he was forced to resign as Shadow Defence Minister after being convicted of being drunk and disorderly during in incident in which he struck a Police officer. And in September last year he, along with 54 other public figures, signed an open letter stating their opposition to the Pope's state visit to the UK. On Sky News on the day after the Lennon attack Foulkes joked that if Celtic moved to the Irish league that would solve the problem.

Bigotry is clearly in the genes too. His son Alex, another Hearts supporter, is a sectarian football hooligan. He was convicted of hurling abuse at Celtic fans – the longest and most sustained police officers had witnessed – and when arrested told the police they'd be in trouble because his father was an MP and his mother was on the police board.

No one would argue that Celtic fans are spotless – one was jailed this week for racial abuse of a Rangers' player – but they have never been guilty of the sustained, anthemic, sectarian chanting and singing that the Rangers support has disgraced itself over more than a century (Rangers will have to play their next European away game supporterless because of it). Their songs are rebel ones about their heritage, rather than foul abuse at the other half of the Old Firm's religion. And it was only in the mid-1980s that Rangers signed its first Catholic player. Pele couldn't have got into the team before then.

It took UEFA, the football authority, to bring the first official sanction on Rangers. Rafts of politicians, councillors and sheriffs could have done it for aeons before, but didn't. And the police have traditionally stood back and allowed the support to 'fuck the Pope' and bathe in 'Fenian blood', despite the flagrant breaches of at least two laws. Only in the last match between the two sides, after what us Scots would call a previous touchline stramash, have the police promised zero tolerance.

Where were they when this crazed numpty, who could have been carrying a knife, jumped over the barrier and launched his attack on Lennon? Given the previous history plod should have been in the dugout with him, or at least hovering in the technical area. And what about the stewards who are meant to stop these incursions? Missing in inaction! Tynecastle, Hearts ground, should now be closed until there are guarantees that such an incident can never re-occur. As should Ibrox, Rangers ground, at the first chirrup of what used to be called a party song but is better described as sectarian bile.

It isn't just the authorities who have been craven over the decades in the face of this, the left are equally guilty. In the wake of the last letter bomb to Lennon I tried to organise an anti-sectarian rally in Glasgow's George Square but my erstwhile political colleagues deliberately scuppered it. There had to be a 'balanced slate', you see, not just Catholics or Celtic supporters – presumably a Church of Scotland minister and a former 'Gers player who had recanted! – because it couldn't just be about the victims. It wasn't intended to be, but why the hell not! If

Lennon had been black or Asian, or a Sighthill asylum seeker they'd have been out on the streets at the drop of a leaflet.

Scottish piety about being a tolerant country has been exploded by the sustained sectarian attacks on Lennon. It's the bigotry which dare not speak its name. To his credit the First Minister Alex Salmond, another Hearts supporter, has condemned the attack. But until there's drastic action against these sick-making Protestant hate-merchants it's just so much mouthwash. We all need to stand behind Neil Lennon. Or, perhaps more accurately, in front of him.

Typical responses....

Gerry Coogan Magnificent, George.

There's hee-haw chance of Scotland sorting out this cancerous hatred of Catholicism and Ireland by itself. It's the default attitude of far too many of them.

One possible starting point though would be to petition UEF...See MoreMay 12 at 9:40pm · 3 people

Sean Stash Callaghan
Spot on george. Shoot from the heartMay 13 at 12:07am

Anti-Catholicism 'deep and wide'

It hasn't gone away. Peter Kearney, director of the Scottish Catholic Media Office, on why sectarianism remains a Scottish problem

Thomas Jefferson, America's third president, claimed that Americans had struggled to be heard by the press and represented fairly in its pages. He wrote in 1807; 'The man who never looks into a newspaper is better informed than he who reads them,' adding, 'inasmuch as he who knows nothing is nearer to truth than he whose mind is filled with falsehoods and errors.'

Reflecting over the coverage of sectarianism in the secular media over the past year, I'd be inclined to agree with Jefferson. Unlike other complaints of intolerance, public charges of anti-Catholicism when made in Scotland are constantly dismissed, doubted and downplayed.

The knee-jerk reaction of too many, journalists, editors and politicians is to portray anti-Catholicism as simply "post-match, drink-fuelled, rivalry" It isn't, it is altogether deeper and wider than that.

At the end of November 2010, I wrote to the Scottish Football Association's Chief Executive, Stewart Regan about an offensive email attacking Pope

Benedict, which had allegedly been sent by a senior SFA official to other SFA staff on 16 September, the day the Pope, visited Scotland. Since no action had been taken in the two months since it was claimed the message had been sent and in the absence of any timetable for action I asked for some urgency and transparency to be brought to bear on the matter.

By the end of the week the official at the centre of the controversy, Hugh Dallas, the Head of Referee Development, had resigned, citing 'family reasons'. While the truths at the heart of this story have yet to emerge, the subject matter shows little sign of disappearing. It is sectarianism in Scotland.

Unfortunately, Scotland has a disturbing track record in this field. Reaction to my intervention proved beyond doubt that Scotland has become completely inured to the corrosive effects of religious bigotry and may even have lost sight of what constitutes it.

Tasteless emails appear to be simply the tip of a disturbing iceberg of anti-Catholicism in Scottish society. Many people have claimed that emails similar to the one in question circulated widely in the weeks leading up to the Pope's visit. These comments are, incredibly, intended to somehow mitigate the culpability of those who were recently being accused. Sadly, they do nothing of the sort. Instead they illuminate what I described in November 2010 as 'a layer of deep, wide and vicious anti Catholic hostility in our country'.

The criticism I faced was designed to deflect attention from the underlying charge of anti-Catholic hostility, which I raised. It is however worth focusing on criticism in order to be better able to respond to it. These are some of the grounds on which I was attacked together with my response to the points made:

• Sectarianism is today a shadow of the problem it once was. Although this is true, particularly in the field of employment, I'm inclined to point out that it does still exist to the detriment of Scottish Catholics. It is also worth remembering that slavery around the world is thankfully a shadow of the problem it once was, but I don't hear anyone suggesting we should turn a blind eye to examples of it as a result.

• By raising complaints of sectarianism you 'fan the flames' of such intolerance and make the problem worse. This is a novel, if nonsensical, criticism. On this basis if all victims of crime and intolerance in Scotland were to remain silent and say nothing of their torments we could transform our Crime Statistics overnight and be "crime-free" within days. It is worth noting, that injunctions to suffer in silence are easier to make than observe.

• Anti-Catholicism cannot exist because many Catholics occupy senior positions in the professions and public life. Again, this is a matter of fact but it simply doesn't undermine the case being made. It is also true that a black man is currently the President of the United States but no one would seriously suggest racism no longer exists in that country.

• Sadly, some Catholics have even claimed that since they have never experienced discrimination or intolerance, it doesn't exist. This is a curious assertion, which amounts to little more than denial of an issue which hasn't been encountered. Few of us, thankfully, have ever had a heroin addiction but that doesn't lead us to deny or doubt that heroin addiction exists and is a problem in Scotland.

• Anti-Catholicism is Scotland's 'default' setting, according to some commentators. Many point out that thousands of offensive emails circulated in the weeks leading up to the Pope's visit, few became public or led to calls for their authors to be dismissed. Incredibly, this 'defence' is actually true! Although it is still startling to think that its truth is seen by some as somehow mitigating the culpability of those who sent offensive messages or endorse intolerance. Like the looter arrested in the middle of a riot whose defence is simply 'everyone else was doing it' it is a hollow and empty objection.

• The Catholic Church has been embroiled recently in a scandalous series of sex abuse cases so Catholics should remain silent. This is tortured logic on a grand scale. Two responses come to mind. Firstly, there are 1.2 billion Catholics in the world. Some of them are venal, corrupt and even criminal. The Catholic Church, in a way not represented in any other organisation on earth, truly represents the broadest sweep of humanity imaginable.

Some Catholic priests, religious and lay people have committed the most heinous and vile crimes. Their behaviour is inexcusable and they should face the fullest punishment the law provides, as should those who have colluded in their crimes. I make no excuses for such behaviour, nor do I defend it. It utterly appals me.

Secondly, I am aware that of the 2,000 or so Catholic priests who have worked in Scotland over the last 25 years less than 0.5 per cent have ever been convicted of sexual abuse. I am disturbed by the fact that in a country where over 99 per cent of Catholic clergy are demonstrably innocent of any offence they can be so frequently subjected to hate-fuelled opprobrium. Ultimately, one case of abuse is one failure too many, but I do not accept for an instant that such failures automatically condemn over one billion people to perpetual silence.

- The Catholic Church has not spoken out on every single instance of anti-Catholic hostility in the past, why therefore make public comments on the Scottish Football Association? This is what you might call the 'all or nothing' approach, it is an innovative, if risible point which is summed up by the dictum, 'If you don't criticise everything, you can't criticise anything'.

- Catholic schools are the root of the problem. This assertion is often made by individuals who are happy to claim that, 'there isn't a problem'! In short Catholics are accused of being the authors of their own destruction via an atavistic compulsion to have their children educated in accordance with their faith. In so doing they sever the otherwise harmonious fabric of Scottish society and introduce separation and difference where none existed. Such nonsense does beg a few questions. First and foremost, what's wrong with difference? Secondly, since anti-Catholicism long predates the existence of Catholic schools surely it can't logically have been caused by them?

Catholic schools exist in dozens of countries around the world, including England, nowhere else are they charged with being the engine of intolerance. Crucially, Catholic schools are not just for Catholics. Between 15 – 20 per cent of the roll in Catholic schools is made up of children of other faiths or of no faith. Muslim parents are particularly supportive and value the ethos and faith-based approach taken. It's also worth noting that while over 95 per cent of Scots Catholics attend Catholic schools over 50 per cent go on to marry non-Catholics, somewhat undermining the fatuous and poisonous canard that schooling leads to lifelong mistrust and separation.

In truth hatred and bigotry are bred in homes not taught in schools. Who can forget the scenes when TV chef Jamie Oliver tried to introduce healthier diets to an English school? As he laboured to improve the dinner menu with salads and nutritious options a gang of mums passed burgers and chips through the playground bars to their children! It's time to stop blaming our teachers and our schools for society's problems.

The pattern which emerges from such objections is clear – when accusations of anti-Catholicism become public, every effort must be made to avoid engaging with them, every barrier must be erected to prevent debate and discussion about the subject itself, no red herring is too small to be thrown into the debate.

The truth is anti-Catholic bigotry has existed in Scotland for a very long time. It existed ten years ago, before any sex abuse revelations had seen the light of day. It was here 20 years ago and 220 years ago. It has existed since the Reformation 450 years ago. Its viciousness was renewed and deepened with the first influx of Irish migrants over a century and a half ago. To pretend otherwise is simply delusional.

Anti-Catholic feeling has often been tolerated by Catholics. A desire to assimilate and integrate has tended to overcome a willingness to challenge. That is changing, I detect a new resolve, especially among younger people not to look the other way or sit at the back of the bus. Our grandparents and even our parents suffered intolerance and persecution. We will not tolerate it. We will not laugh it off or see the funny side - because there is no funny side. Beneath the surface of the nasty emails and the intemperate asides of public figures there are others whose malignancy is altogether more pernicious.

As the racist bile of 'comedians' like Bernard Manning underpinned and affirmed the actions of many who committed racially motivated attacks in the 1970s and 80s so too does the Catholic baiting of the chattering classes bolster the bigotry of a new generation of vicious thugs. They are the ones who threw the concrete block at the Lanarkshire priest, striking him in the head.

They are the ones who surrounded the car of the West Lothian priest hurling vile invective at him and trapping him in fear. They are the ones who hurled a brick through the bedroom window of the Renfrewshire priest as he slept. These are a mere snapshot of the daily tide of intolerance Catholics, especially clergy, have suffered and continue to suffer in what was once dubbed 'the best small country in the world'. An epithet quickly re-coined by some exasperated Catholics as 'the best small-minded country in the world'.

That sectarianism continues to dominate the Scottish news agenda recently should not surprise anyone. That public debate on the matter continues to comprise, almost without exception, fatuous, ill informed and hackneyed drivel is however quite shocking. That lives can be threatened with bombs and bullets is utterly chilling.

So what can be done, what action can be taken? Since 2003 when Section 74 of that year's Criminal Justice Scotland Act created the offence of Aggravated Sectarianism, Scotland has been trying to tackle this problem with one hand tied behind its back. The sustained refusal by the Crown Office to publish a detailed breakdown of sectarian-motivated crime is nothing short of outrageous.

Their inaction has prevented, politicians, the police and Scottish society from tackling religious intolerance and from having an informed debate on the subject. In the absence of detail on such offences being available in the public domain, the facile dogmas of 'one side's as bad as the other' have prevailed, as have the demonstrably false assertions that sectarianism is all about football or reserved to the West of Scotland.

For over four years the Catholic Church has been calling for a detailed breakdown of the statistics. Cardinal O'Brien led calls for such a release in 2006 at the second 'National Sectarianism Summit', political action was promised but none followed. Interestingly, prior to the summit the Crown Office did release a detailed breakdown of the offence and its use.

An analysis by the Catholic Media Office showed that Catholics were five times more likely to suffer a sectarian attack than anyone else. This analysis was circulated widely to the media. Thereafter the detailed breakdowns stopped and have never been published since.

Further compounding the problem is the fact that over the course of a single generation, Scotland's political, academic and media elite have almost completely lost contact with religious practice and belief. This derogation from universally held objective moral standards supplanted by the embrace of subjective secular fashions has brought with it catastrophic consequences. Among them is the creation of a generation of decision makers who flail helplessly when trying to understand the nuances of religiously-motivated crime without admitting that they are spectacularly ill-equipped to do so.

Sadly, for the most part Scottish sectarianism comprises; widespread, sustained and virulent anti-Catholicism. It cannot be tackled until this truth is acknowledged. Full publication of the Section 74 statistics must be the beginning of an open and informed debate, it must lead to far greater transparency on the part of the police and the prosecuting authorities.

But it is only a beginning. Behind the detail of a few hundred convictions each year lies an iceberg of intolerance. For every offender convicted of an offence 'aggravated by religious prejudice' there are many more whose 'aggravated' charge will have been bargained by fiscals and defence lawyers to secure a conviction on the primary charge.

Equally for everyone charged with sectarian crime, there are many more who commit such crimes and are never charged. I have lost count of the number of priests who've had windows broken, buildings vandalised and insults hurled at them, yet despite my encouragement they are reluctant to involve the police or the media in their torments for fear of inviting reprisals or copycat attacks.

This background bigotry, which blights so many lives, is never registered in official statistics, it is rarely recorded and hardly ever reported – what action plan exists to tackle and eradicate it?

When we speak of eradicating sectarianism from Scotland we don't define our goal in any detail. We may simply mean we should enjoy a year in which no sectarian crimes are committed. Yet what of the hatred and intolerance that lives on in so many hearts and minds?

We will truly have eradicated anti-Catholic sectarianism from our society when newspaper editors stop commissioning articles which argue for the abolition of Catholic schools, when teaching unions stop passing similarly intolerant resolutions and when Scotland's education system reflects the plurality of faiths found in society.

Why should tax-paying parents who follow a secular humanist belief system be denied the opportunity to have their children educated in accordance with their beliefs, or for that matter Muslim parents?

I've yet to meet a parent who believes in 'nothing'.

Everyone I've ever encountered has a set of beliefs of one kind or another, there is no mythical default setting, despite what secular humanists might tell us and so there can never be an equitable 'one size fits all' education system.

Over the last 10 years significant amounts of public money has been given to organisations offering anti-sectarianism training and information. Most, if not all, Scottish schoolchildren have been given talks, workshops and leaflets on the subject. Using the measurable criteria we have there is no indication to date that the problem has diminished. This may be an appropriate time therefore to question the merits of public funding for 'one-size-fits-all' anti-intolerance programmes. It seems reasonable to question their efficacy and examine their value. Such approaches unless carefully focused on a measurable problem, can often reduce to nothing more than lowest common denominator platitudes.

Equally, politicians and police forces should use specific terminology and directly address the problem of anti-Catholicism. In the same way that annual drink-drive purges aren't referred to as road safety campaigns but specifically labelled in accordance with the behaviour they seek to eradicate, so too should anti-sectarianism initiatives be labelled in a far more specific way.

We must seize the chance to adopt an evidence-based approach from now on. When the Crown Office produced an analysis of sectarian crime on 2006 the detail was instructive. If conviction statistics show that Catholics are still six times more likely to suffer sectarian attacks then targeted action with the support of the Catholic community must be the response. If the data continues to reveal that 85 per cent of sectarian crime is not football-related then the 'football summits' should end and the incessant focus on club's behaviour should change to a wider review of society and the development of a truly respectful culture of religious tolerance.

Last but by no means least in the list of action which could be taken to signal real intent on the part of the state to deal with sectarianism would be the repeal of the Act of Settlement. It is archaic, anachronistic and discriminatory, it is everything we claim as a modern and tolerant society to reject and it should go.

Interestingly, the SNP policy of retaining the Queen as the Head of State of an independent Scotland could see Scotland's ability to remove this repugnant relic, diminished. It is to be hoped that the quid pro quo for retention of the monarchy would be repeal of the act. A future Scotland with no MPs at Westminster and a perpetually anti-Catholic constitution would still be in no position to preach religious tolerance successfully!

It is worth remembering, that Catholics do not represent intemperate or extreme zealotry. We do not call for persecution of any kind to be shown to those who do not share our beliefs. I have many friends of other faiths and Christian traditions, I respect their beliefs completely as they do mine. I am however a member of a generation formed and nurtured in Scotland to play a full and active part in the life and future of this country. I will not allow that entitlement to be questioned, disparaged, demeaned or besmirched in any way.

Let no one be in any doubt, the shameful bigotry of the past year has caused many Catholics in Scotland to draw a line in the sand. The bigotry, the bile, the sectarian undercurrents and innuendos must end. Such hateful attitudes have had their day, they poison the well of community life, they must be excised and cast out once and for all.

Lennon's troubles. The timeline

March 1, 2001 Lennon, who had signed for Celtic three months earlier, considers retiring from international football after being booed by Northern Ireland fans during defeat by Norway at Windsor Park in Belfast.

Aug 21, 2002 Pulls out of the Northern Ireland team on the evening of a match against Cyprus after receiving a death threat from a paramilitary group. The threat was made by telephone to the BBC.

May 8, 2003 Attacked close to his home in Glasgow's West End after stopping in his car at a red light and being abused. Two students are later fined after admitting a breach of the peace.

Sept 1, 2008 Requires hospital treatment after being

attacked and knocked unconscious in the West End after Celtic's Old Firm derby defeat. Two Rangers fans are later jailed for assault.

Jan 5, 2011 A package addressed to Lennon, by now the Celtic manager, and containing bullets, is intercepted at a sorting office in Mallusk, County Antrim. Irish player Niall McGinn is also targeted.

March 2, 2011 Involved in heated exchanges with Rangers player El Hadji Diouf and assistant manager Ally McCoist on the touchline during Celtic's Scottish Cup win at Parkhead. Receives four-match ban.

April 19, 2011 It emerges that Royal Mail intercepted a total of two 'viable' liquid-based parcel bombs addressed to Lennon. High-profile Celtic fans Trish Godman and Paul McBride QC were also targeted.

May 11, 2011 Lennon is attacked by a fan on the touchline during Celtic's 3-0 win against Hearts at Tynecastle. The fan climbs out of the Hearts section to accost Lennon and is then taken away by police. The Hearts fan John Wilson is charged over the attack.

Sectarian abuse at Windsor Park

Neil Lennon, playing for Northern Ireland, is booed every time he touches the ball in the 4-0 defeat by

Norway in a supposed friendly match and leaves the field at half-time.

Lennon, who had recently signed for Celtic and was making his 36th appearance, was so upset he left the ground immediately.

Loyalist bigots targeted the midfielder because of his signing for Celtic and a couple of days before had daubed 'Neil Lennon RIP' on a wall in Lisburn.

Lennon had previously said he would like to play for an all-Ireland team which turns him into a hate figure for the Orange bigots. The crowd is overwhelmingly Protestant but many of the fans reacted to the boos by cheering Lennon and chanting 'One Neil Lennon'. This means, bizarrely, that each time Lennon touches the ball he is jeered and cheered simultaneously.

He is spared any further anguish when manager Sammy McIlroy decides to take him off and replaces him with Dundee United's Danny Griffin.

'In the main, the reception I received was brilliant,' says Lennon. 'A lot of people got behind me tonight and I was touched by that. There are minorities in all walks of like who make trouble for everyone else. But there are a lot more good people than bad in this country.

'I hope to be back but first I will talk things over with my club and family and take it from there.'

The Irish Football Association is hugely embarrassed by the incident after it has recently launched an anti-sectarianism campaign. Their slogan was 'Football 1 Sectarianism 0'

Lennon quits international team

The Guardian reports that football in Northern Ireland is plunged into a sectarian crisis after team captain Neil Lennon is forced to pull out of the friendly match with Cyprus after receiving death threats.

Lennon, who is due to captain his country in the match at Windsor Park, tolls his international manager Sammy McIlroy of his decision just hours before kick-off after police had earlier informed him of the threats.

Lennon continued to play for his country after his family in Lurgan received threats following his transfer from Leicester City to Celtic.

Irish Football Association general secretary, David Bowen, confirms the player's withdrawal. 'Police informed Neil of a threat earlier today. The manager spoke to Neil and Neil spoke to his family and others and for family reasons he has told us that he has had to withdraw from tonight's game.'

Irish Football Association president Jim Boyce says he could understand the Lennon's decision, but questioned how football in Northern Ireland could deal with such sectarianism. 'No one knows if this is serious or a crank, but at the end of the day I have to respect the player's views,' he says.

'This is just unbelievable. It is a terrible blight once again on society in Northern Ireland, especially when you think of the efforts made by the Irish Football Association to stamp this sort of thing out.'

Three men sought for attack

Lennon, now 31, is attacked at a set of traffic lights in the Hillhead area of Glasgow during the early hours.

Police issue descriptions of three men they want to question after the assault.

Lennon is sitting in his car when he is approached by three men who shout abuse at him. He and a female companion drive off but the car is chased by the men who kick it at traffic lights.

When he gets out of the car he is assaulted, suffering slight injuries. His female friend, who is pushed over, is shaken but unhurt.

Lennon has now retired from international football after receiving death threats before the match.

Police say they cannot not rule out the possibility that the assault was sectarian. Two Glasgow University students are convicted.

Hospitalised after attack

The former Celtic captain and now coach is knocked unconscious and hospitalised by a street attack just hours after Rangers' Old Firm victory.

Police inquiries are continuing into the incident, which occurs after Lennon leaves a bar close to his home in Glasgow's West End. The 37-year-old suffers facial injuries and concussion from what appears to have been an unprovoked attack by two men just after midnight, before receiving treatment in the city's Western Infirmary.

Strathclyde police say in a statement: 'We can confirm police were called to a report of a 37-year-old man being assaulted in Ashton Lane. The injured man was taken to hospital and discharged after treatment for minor injuries. He did not wish to make a complaint.'

A Celtic statement adds: 'The assault came after Neil was subjected to sectarian abuse. It is understood that during the course of the attack Neil lost consciousness.'

Two Rangers' fans are subsequently arrested, convicted and jailed.

Lennon and others sent bullets

Packages containing bullets are sent from Northern Ireland to the Celtic manager Neil Lennon and player Niall McGinn.

The packages, addressed to the two men, are intercepted by staff at the Royal Mail sorting office in Mallusk, County Antrim. The mail is bound for Celtic Park.

Police in Northern Ireland say officers were called to Mallusk office on 5 January after postal workers report suspicions about two items of mail. The items are removed for further examination, and police continue to investigate the incident.

Lennon and McCoist square up

Lennon and Rangers assistant Ally McCoist shake hands at full time. But Lennon then appears to react angrily to something said by McCoist. After pointing his finger in McCoist's face, Lennon is pulled away and McCoist is ushered down the tunnel.

The clash comes at the end of a bitterly-contested derby, even by Old Firm standards, in which three Rangers players are sent off. Steven Whittaker and Madjid Bougherra are dismissed - both for second bookings - during the game and El-Hadji Diouf is dismissed after full time.

Parcel bombs sent to Lennon

A package addressed to Lennon is intercepted at the Royal Mail sorting office in Kirkintilloch, East Dunbartonshire, on 26 March.

Another parcel for Scottish politician Trish Godman was intercepted at her constituency office and on 15 April a package was also intercepted en route to Paul McBride, who has represented Lennon during his dispute with the Scottish Football Association.

Police confirm that all three packages contained viable bombs

They are subsequently traced to a post box in Kilwinning and two men are arrested and charged. At the time of writing they have still not faced trial.

Lennon attacked by Hearts fan

Four minutes into the second half, with Gary Hooper having scored his second goal in Celtic's 3-0 win, a spectator suddenly vaults the barrier separating the Hearts fans behind the Celtic technical area from the pitch, and throws himself at Lennon.

He is almost immediately smothered by stewards

and police – not before the incensed Lennon has swung a kick at him – and dragged down the tunnel. It's taken for granted that the Scottish Football Association demands to know how it was possible that a figure such as Lennon – who has been the subject of threats and who was the intended recipient of a mail bomb in April – could not depend on the host club to secure the technical area.

Scottish First Minister Salmond says: 'This sort of behaviour is utterly unacceptable. The Joint Action Group formed after the recent football summit is developing the eight-point plan to present to ministers before the start of the new season to tackle all issues of violence and bigotry in relation to football, because we cannot have the safety of individuals endangered by such mindless incidents, and our national game tarnished.'

Celtic's assistant manager, Johan Mjallby, says he would not blame Lennon for walking away from football after this latest incident. 'What has happened to Neil is a dark day for Scottish football. I haven't really had time to speak to Neil, he has a strong character but how much can one guy take? The backroom staff are desperate for him to continue but no one could blame him if he decided not to,' he said.

'I was watching out of the corner of my eye and Thommo [coach Alan Thompson] reacted. Neil Lennon defended himself, of course he would. I'm shocked and Neil must be even more afraid. What if he had something in his hand? We all have to look into this, a manager should be secure inside a football ground.'

And also - U-17 Berwick Rangers Captain sacked over Neil Lennon death wish comments

Kieran Bowell (*sic*) sacked for comments made on the social networking site Twitter about the bombs sent to Neil Lennon. The Third Division side released a statement on their official website, stating that the player's contract has been 'terminated with immediate effect'. The post on Twitter read, *"Wish that parcel bomb f****** killed neil lennon, the little c***."*

A second footballer is then sacked for comments made on the social networking site Twitter about Lennon.

Max McKee, an Under-19 player with Clyde FC, has his contract terminated with immediate effect. McKee tweeted a message saying, *"Somebody needs to hurry up and shoot Neil Lennon #JustSaying."*

Two other youth players are under investigation by their clubs – St.Mirren and Motherwell – for comments on their social networking sites.

Another youth player in Scottish Football, Under-19 Partick Thistle player Derek Hepburn, is caught making sectarian and racist remarks, on top of comments in relation to the recent attacks on Neil Lennon, on the social networking site Facebook. His comments go back as far as January! Hepburn is the FIFTH Youth player in Scotland to be caught making sick and vile remarks. However unlike the rest, Hepburn's sustained attacks are not a one-off, and are sectarian in their tone also.

heraldscotland

Thursday 28 July 2011 The Herald | sundayherald

WEATHER
Edinburgh 15.8°C
▶ Change location

Police: Rangers fans can sing The Sash

GERRY BRAIDEN

28 Jul 2011

THE Scottish Government's plans to tackle sectarianism ran into fresh controversy last night after it emerged Rangers fans have been told they will not be arrested for singing Loyalist anthem The Sash.

Supporters' groups met police and club officials this week to discuss acceptable singing during games at Ibrox and were told songs like The Sash and Build My Gallows would be allowed as they contain no sectarian references. But the decision is likely to cause controversy as many Catholics consider the songs inflammatory.

Andy Kerr, president of the Rangers Supporters' Assembly, said: "Essentially at this stage it's what song is going to get you arrested and the club into trouble and what won't and we've got clarification on that from the police." He added there was an upsurge in fans apprehending other Rangers fans indulging in sectarian behaviour.

At this week's meeting it was also agreed to continue 'self-policing' and to 'continue to ask that fans eradicate all singing of The Billy Boys and derogatory references to Catholics".

The decision comes in the wake of a Government pledge to tackle sectarianism. Initial proposals were shelved amid difficulties with enforcement when it emerged that fans could be prosecuted for crossing themselves or singing God Save The Queen.

Strathclyde Police said officers who attended the meetings were unavailable for comment but a source said: "Singing The Sash as a rule will not get you arrested but fans should ask themselves whether it's appropriate to sing these songs at a football match."

Loyalists' matchday parades will go ahead

GERRY BRAIDEN

28 Jul 2011

CONTROVERSIAL Loyalist parades planned for the immediate vicinity of Celtic Park on matchday will go ahead after organisers and the police agreed to early start times and shorter routes, The Herald understands.

The compromise between the Royal Black Chapter, a cousin of the Orange Order, and Strathclyde Police will be ratified by Glasgow City Council this afternoon, a fortnight before the intended parade.

Earlier proposals by the Royal Black Chapter for a later parade were refused as a new policy by the city council forbids processions playing music after 6pm, while the police were concerned about being overstretched on a Saturday evening.

The organisation had intended to stage simultaneous processions along Duke Street in Glasgow's east end on Saturday, August 13, less than half-an-hour after the final whistle of the match between Celtic and Dundee United, when up to 60,000 supporters would be spilling out of the ground.

The parades, commemorating the 322nd anniversary of The Relief of Derry during the Williamite wars in Ireland, also clash with the World Pipe Band Championships, with police warning that proximity to Celtic Park "introduces an unacceptable risk in relation to public order, traffic and pedestrian congestion".

It takes a man to stand

The 2010/11 football season in Scotland was the most memorably shocking one in living memory. The beautiful game was besmirched, disgraced and scandalised.

It began with the controversy and furore that emerged following Celtic's match against Dundee United at Tannadice in November 2010, during which referee Dougie McDonald awarded a penalty to Celtic only to then rescind it after consulting with his assistant, Steven Craven.

It was later revealed that McDonald colluded with Referees Development Head, Hugh Dallas, already a controversial figure where Celtic are concerned, to lie to the Celtic manager over the reason for giving the penalty in the first place. Referee's assistant Steven Craven resigned a few days later, as did Dougie McDonald after Neil Lennon came out publicly saying that he should follow suit.

The following week, after the Old Firm derby, Celtic wrote to the SFA querying the penalty that was awarded to Rangers by the referee in that game, Willie Collum. This prompted the unprecedented prospect of strike action by Scottish referees, protesting at what they viewed as their integrity being called into question by the actions of Celtic, and more specifically, Celtic manager Neil Lennon. Matters weren't helped when Lennon was slapped with a draconian six-game touchline ban after a confrontation with the fourth official during Celtic's match against Hearts at Tynecastle a few weeks later.

A few days before the planned strike by Scottish referees, Hugh Dallas was forced to resign when it came to light that he'd sent a derogatory and offensive email about the Pope prior to his visit to Scotland in 2010. Peter Kearney of the Scottish Catholic Media Office described the email as an example of 'deep, wide and vicious anti-Catholic hostility,' and was just the 'tip of the iceberg' of anti-Catholic sentiment in Scotland.

Yet despite Hugh Dallas's email, despite the scandal surrounding the penalty award at Tannadice involving Dallas prior to it coming to light, and despite the fact that the referee and referee's assistant who were involved in the penalty scandal had resigned, the majority of Scottish football writers, commentators and journalists in general blamed Celtic and Neil Lennon for the subsequent referee's strike.

Celtic, to their credit, remained unrepentant, citing the penalty incident involving referee Dougie McDonald and SFA refereeing official Hugh Dallas in an attempted cover-up.

Going into January 2011 things were tense as a series of Old Firm fixtures approached. The fourth of these, a Scottish Cup tie replay at Celtic Park, exploded into ugly confrontation on the park between the players and on the touchline between Ally McCoist and Neil Lennon. Inexplicably, at least for those who still harboured faith in the SFA as an honest and objective arbiter of the game, McCoist was given a two-match ban while Lennon was handed down a four-match ban for the very same incident, which as the TV footage shows was clearly instigated by McCoist. Rangers immediately appealed McCoist's ban, with the result that it was quashed.

Meanwhile, two Rangers players involved in on the field incidents and who were sent off for misconduct, El Hadji Diouf and Madjid Bougherra, were given no ban whatsoever and received token fines.

This prompted a statement by Neil Lennon and Celtic's lawyer, Paul McBride QC: 'The SFA are officially the laughing stock of world football and they have been shown to be not merely dysfunctional and not merely dishonest but biased because McCoist, who undoubtedly said something that provoked a reaction from Neil Lennon that caused a four-match ban for him, has received no punishment at all.'

Meanwhile, Scotland's First Minister, Alex Salmond, convened a summit involving the Scottish government, Strathclyde Police and officials from both Old Firm clubs, designed to ensure that the events that took place during the Old Firm match at Celtic Park would never take place again, citing the number of arrests that took place both inside and outside the ground as an indication that things had got out of control.

In January 2011, prior to this controversy, Neil Lennon along with two Celtic and Republic of Ireland players, Niall McGinn and Paddy McCourt, received live bullets in the post. This was followed by the attempt to send mail bombs to Lennon, Paul McBride, and Trish Godman three months later, a further bomb intended for the Glasgow-based Irish cultural association Cairde N'Eireann (Friends of Ireland) also intercepted. It was followed by a touchline attack on Lennon at Tynecastle Park as the season drew to a close, when, as mentioned elsewhere a Hearts fan managed to get onto the pitch intent on doing the Celtic manager physical harm.

There have been many who have attempted to dismiss the attempt to kill and/or maim the intended recipients of these devices as just the work of a 'few nutters' unrepresentative of any wider societal or cultural manifestation of anti-Irish Catholic bigotry and racism. Indeed, religious sectarianism is no longer a major problem in Scottish society, they argue, confined nowadays to the '90 minute' bigots who fill the stands at Ibrox and Celtic Park.

Unfortunately for them this assertion is contradicted by the facts – quite literally in the form of recent sets of statistics which reveal that in areas such as crime and social exclusion Catholics fare worse than any other demographic.

As recently as January 2011 the Scottish Prison Service released figures revealing that almost 30 per cent of the nation's prison population are Catholics, nearly double the percentage of Catholics in the population as a whole, which currently stands at 16 percent.

Furthermore, back in 2007, the leader of the Catholic Church in Scotland, Cardinal Keith O'Brien, himself the recipient of a live bullet in the post in 2010, led calls for a government investigation into the findings of a census which revealed that 19 per cent of the country's Catholic population occupied 10 percent of the most deprived housing areas, compared to 14 per cent of Muslims and eight per cent who described themselves as Church of Scotland.

From the same census, the findings of which were published in 2005, the cardinal also seized on the fact that out of 726 documented cases of sectarian-motivated abuse or assault in Scotland between 2004 and 2005, 64 per cent of the victims were Catholics. At the time the Cardinal's spokesman said:

It is a matter of some concern that Catholics are disproportionately represented in Scotland's prison population and are more likely to occupy the poorest-quality housing. Wider research on these phenomena would be very helpful in attempting to ascertain what, if any, social trends underpin such disadvantage.

It is precisely this lack of wider research that gives cause for concern. Why has this been the case? Is it because the conclusions of any such research would embarrass the powers that be as to the extent and nature of the problem – i.e. the extent of anti Roman Catholic bigotry and anti Irish racism that exists in Scotland? Has this resulted in a lack of political will to grasp the nettle and tackle the issue at its roots?

It would seem so.

Since 2006 the Scottish government and the Crown Office have refused repeated requests for a breakdown of the character of sectarian crimes. Under Section 74 of the Criminal Justice Act (2003), individuals can be convicted for religiously aggravated offences. While the Crown Office publishes the total number of convictions under Section 74 every year, it refuses to reveal how many crimes were anti-Catholic, anti-Protestant, antisemitic or anti-Muslim. In other words while we may have a grasp of the size of the problem, we remain in the dark when it comes to its trend. The last published figures which included such a breakdown are as mentioned from 2005.

This means that at as I write it has been five years since the data surrounding religious sectarianism has been properly quantified, which to put it mildly is simply not good enough.

Along with the Catholic Church, I question the political will to tackle this issue on the part of the political and legal establishment in Scotland. Along with leading academics, I also question how Scotland can even begin to deal with the problem if vital statistics are being withheld.

The official reason given by the government and the Crown Office for this failure is that retrieving the data is too time-consuming and complicated. I'm sorry, but this garbage. In fact worse than garbage it is a gross insult to the victims and will only succeed in ensuring there are more victims rather than less going forward.

In the wake of the spate of mail bombs that were intercepted at the beginning of 2011, and the racist and bigoted campaign to drive Neil Lennon out of Scotland, the SNP said they would publish a detailed analysis if re-elected. Well, they have been re-elected, so let's see some action. Let's have the figures and start by acknowledging the nature of the problem – namely that in Scotland anti-Irish racism and anti-Catholic bigotry is the truth that dare not speak its name.

Anything less is political cowardice, further evidence of the institutional apathy when it comes to an issue which is rightly described as Scotland's shame.

The SNP are fond of promoting Scottish independence as a progressive advance for the Scottish people. I say to them now, and to all supporters of independence, that until the roots of anti-Catholic bigotry and anti-Irish racism have been removed, the words progressive and Scotland do not belong in the same sentence. Yes, the SNP government did try to introduce an anti-sectarianism act in time for the new football season, but that turned from well-intentioned, to farce and then collapse. But more of that elsewhere.

This brings me back to Neil Lennon, the victim of a sustained and unrelenting hate campaign ever since arriving at Celtic as a player in the year 2000.

The reason why he has always been a hate figure for the bigots and racists is simply because he refuses to bend the knee or shift his eyes down in deference to the dominant culture. He is in other words the embodiment of the difference between passivity and defiance in the face of oppression.

Anyone can sit. An old woman can sit. A coward can sit. ... It takes a man to stand.

Those were the words of a great hero of mine, Malcolm X, when describing the difference between passivity and defiance in the struggle for freedom for blacks in the United States during the sixties; between those who adopted the tactics of sit down protests, allowing themselves to be beaten without a fight, and those like him who advocated defending themselves.

Neil Lennon typifies the defiant approach, despite those who, betraying their own lack of courage and principle when it comes to confronting racism and bigotry, accuse him of bringing it on himself in daring to stand and look his tormenters in the eye. In contrast to many who watched the final Rangers v Celtic of the 2010/11 season at Ibrox, when Lennon cupped his ears to the Rangers faithful as he walked off the pitch, after paying his customary tribute to the Celtic fans, I was proud of him – proud of his courage in refusing to be cowed or intimidated in the face of repeated threats and an actual attempt on his life for no other reason than he happens to be proud of his culture and ethnicity - Catholic and Irish - and proud of his association with an institution that represents both.

'I'd hope all of that is behind me,' Neil said characteristically, reflecting on the events. 'I don't want to be a cause, I want to be a good manager. I want to be thought of and respected as that.'

I have written this book in tribute to the courage of Neil Lennon, who for me belongs in the same company as those who throughout history have chosen to stand rather than sit when confronted by racism and oppression.

Me? I stand with him.

What about you?

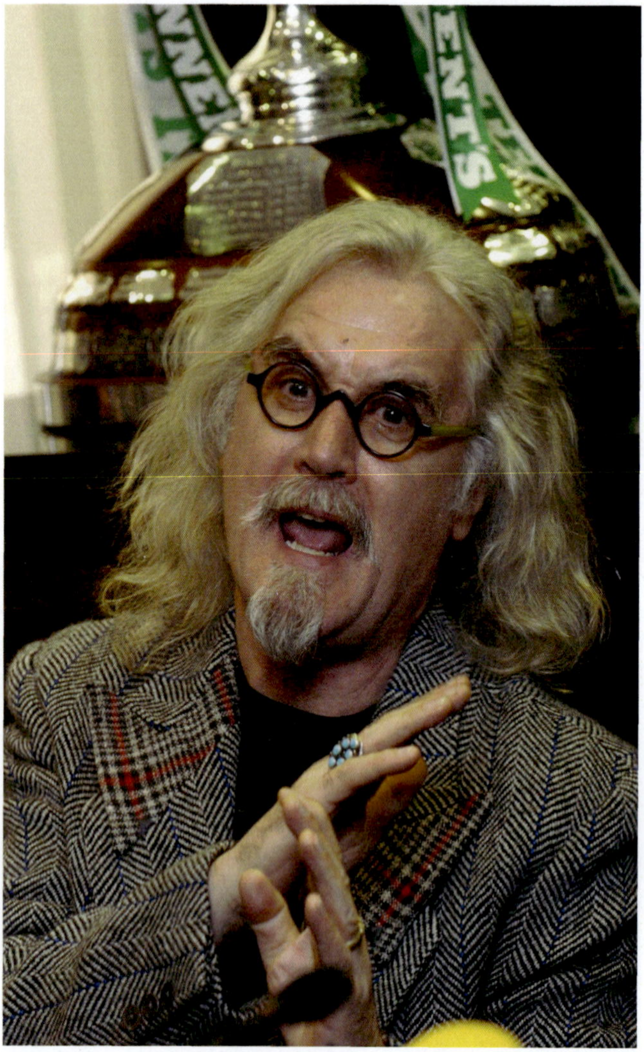

The Big Yin on the Great Yin

Neil Lennon....Ahhh Neil Lennon, he'd be a useful guy. He doesn't get any credit. To me he's a great hero, and off the park as well for what he has stood up to. When they talk about the anti-bigotry campaign Rangers supporters can sing the sash their father wore 'til I'm blue in the face. I don't really care. I don't think that's where the problem is. I think the problem with bigotry is where people won't give people houses and won't give people jobs and stuff like that. Or to broadcasters who are on Saturday or Sunday sports programmes and when they're on and people say "why is Neil Lennon being booed?" they say "I don't know why," when they do know.

They could cut to the chase, they could be so instrumental in cutting this crap...It's the don't knows. I have a go at them on stage. Well, I say, I do know. I know exactly why. How come you don/t know and you're in broadcasting? Maybe you should resign if there's something you don't know that everyone else knows?

George Galloway and Paul McBride

Age-old prejudices tolerated

Paul McBride is Neil Lennon's lawyer. And he is, to me, the bravest lawman in the land, a man who speaks his mind without hesitation or fear. Many thought he went too far in defending Celtic during open season given his professional position and status. Maybe he did. But the important thing is that he did because as a man of principle he could do no other.

And that's another thing that sets McBride apart. He stands for something. And even when those things are different from what I believe in, his willingness to speak up and stand up is something I respect. If you're his friend he will never turn away in times of trouble, as Neil Lennon found last season at the height of the campaign to drive him out of Scotland.

His stance earned him a bomb in the post, which by the grace of God failed in its objective of ending his life. I was glad to be able to interview him for Open Season. Some said he wouldn't do it. Too controversial, they said. They don't know Paul McBride.

GG: First of all Paul, thanks for agreeing to this interview, especially as I know that as one of the most sought after QCs in the country your time is precious.

PM: No problem, George. In fact it's my pleasure. It's an important issue. Thank you for inviting me.

GG: Paul, let me begin by asking you what your feelings are on last season's events four months on? What comes to mind when you reflect on what took place?

PM: My earnest hope when I consider what took place last season is that we never see anything like it again. I hope that this season is remembered for football and nothing else. The most striking thing for me is how these disgusting events shamed not only Scottish football but Scotland as a nation.

GG: What's been your impression of the political response to these events? Has it been robust and coherent enough in your view?

PM: Well, like you I am not a supporter of the SNP.

But I have to say I've been impressed with their attempt to get a handle on this, which is something I'm afraid I can't say for the other major parties in Scotland.

The legislation proposed by the SNP that was meant to be in place by the start of this season has been put back at the behest of the other parties on the basis that they required more time to consider the whys and wherefores.

Let me be kind and describe this as unfortunate. It is illustrative of the vacillation and lack of courage when it comes to dealing with this issue in Scotland. The offence was committed now and to my mind there has been no compelling reason to delay the implementation of legislation other than a desire to sweep the issue under the carpet.

I'm also bound to say that the appointment of Roseanna Cunningham in the newly established post of Minister of Community Safety and Legal Affairs, with a particular remit to tackle sectarianism, is a positive step forward.

GG: Yes, let's hope so, especially as it has long been my belief that when it comes to tackling bigotry and its root causes in Scotland, politicians and opinion formers have been guilty of running scared. Do you think this will ever change? If so, what will it take?

PM: I agree with your point about the historical failure of our politicians to get to grips with this cancer at the heart of our society. The problem is that apart from very few exceptions, yourself included, we have a political culture whereby reacting to events rather than seeking to provide leadership in response to them is endemic.

An example of the latter was your stance on the war in Iraq. You invited a lot of hostility and calumny for the stance you took from the start, including being ejected from the party you'd been a member of your entire political life. Yet now, almost a decade on, there's hardly a person in the land who would disagree with your views on the war and on Tony Blair, I imagine.

By the way, I remain one of the few who still disagrees with you on the war. But that's another interview.

GG: Ha-ha, indeed. Scotland likes to view itself as a friendly, progressive society, and certainly the SNP government promotes Scotland as a forward thinking country that will flourish if independent. In light of last season's events would you agree with me that until anti-Irish Catholic racism and bigotry is dealt with properly the words Scottish independence and progressive will remain a contradiction?

PM: Absolutely. I think there are legitimate concerns on the part of Scotland's Catholic community that if Scotland were ever to become independent and these prejudices remained as deep and wide as they evidently are, it could result in very serious consequences when it comes to social cohesion and related matters.

We mustn't delude ourselves that this isn't the most serious social issue in the country today. If we do, if we continue to treat it with the collective myopia it has been traditionally treated with, we will only succeed in failing future generations.

GG: Moving on to Neil Lennon, I think that throughout the hate campaign he's endured, which I'll repeat has been undertaken with the objective of driving him and his family out of Scotland, he acquitted himself with enormous courage and dignity. What do you think?

PM: I really couldn't agree more. Neil has displayed extraordinary courage. I mean, despite being forced to deal with a serious attempt on his life, being assaulted in the dugout, his family being threatened and having to live surrounded by security, he still took Celtic from nowhere to winning a trophy and one point short of winning the league.

I'll never forget being at Celtic Park on the last home game of the season. The atmosphere was just unbelievable. In fact you'd think we'd just won the Champions League.

It was an atmosphere of defiance and unity in the face of adversity, which was down to Neil Lennon and the courage he demonstrated. In fact, he succeeded in unifying the club in a way I've never seen since I've been a supporter and associated with the club.

GG: Yes, I attended a few home games last season myself and have to say that the atmosphere at Celtic Park was extraordinary.

Changing tack slightly, I don't think the buck stops with Scottish football on this. And I reject the thesis of the 90 minute bigot that's been put forward by some to explain the nature of the problem in some of our grounds when it comes to the singing of sectarian songs and anti-Irish Catholic bigotry. I believe it runs deeper than that, much deeper in fact.

PM: I agree. One of the most striking aspects of last season's events for me was the dilatory response from the Orange Order, the SFA and even the Church of Scotland. To say they were slow in coming out in condemnation is an understatement. I mean, it was only 20 years ago that Rangers signed a Catholic.

Personally, I found when it came to various emails I read within the SFA, with the revelations of statements made by high profile officials in the game, that these negative attitudes and prejudices are still being tolerated.

The quote that 'evil flourishes when good men stand back and do nothing' comes to mind. I'm afraid that this is exactly what I found last season.

GG: I describe in the book how my attempt to organise an anti-sectarian public rally in Glasgow at the height of these events was stymied and undermined by various individuals and organisations who if it had been Muslims or asylum seekers would have been hitting the streets with the placards without having to be asked twice – and rightly so. What do you think the impact of a public rally would have been?

PM: It's hard to know what the impact would have been. But we have had glimpses of the potential for both sides of this chasm to come together. I'm thinking specifically here of what happened when Tommy

Burns died and you had Walter Smith and Ally McCoist helping to carry his coffin into the chapel, and how Celtic and Rangers supporters paid their respects together and were able to put to one side any animosity or acrimony over their differences.

At the end of the day what unites us is far stronger than anything that divides us. Twenty years ago homophobia and racism were more or less tolerated within Scottish society. Now they're not.

This was the result of people refusing to tolerate these prejudices and backward attitudes any longer, rather than burying their heads in the sand and just hoping they would disappear. A rally against homophobia would have been unthinkable 20 years ago. Not now.

GG: Finally, Paul, on a personal level has the experience of being the intended recipient of one of these mail bombs because of your links to Neil Lennon and Celtic had any bearing on how you lead your life now?

PM: Certainly not. In fact if anything it has made me determined not to change a thing when it comes to how I live or go about my day to day activities. I am proud to be associated with Celtic and my affiliation to the club will not change one bit. No, I can assure you, I will not be cowed, and neither should anybody else associated with the club. After all, it's a Grand Old Team To Play For.

GG: Hear, Hear. Or more to the point - Hail, Hail!

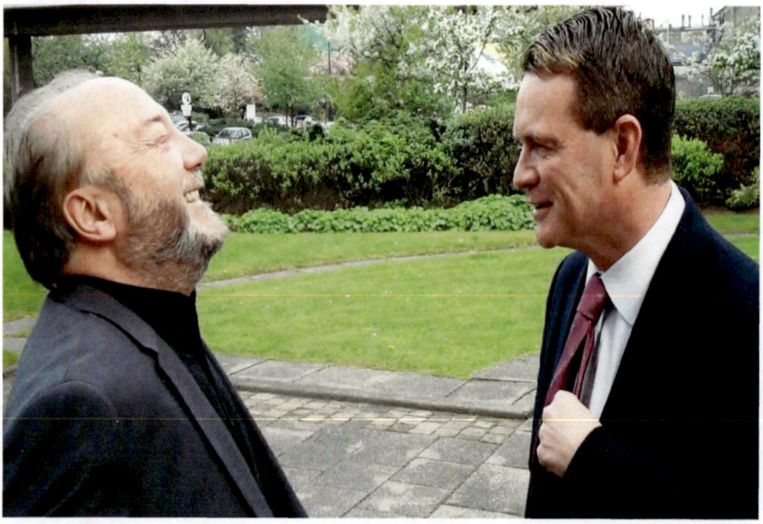

The John Wilson 'trial'

Thousands of fans inside Tynecastle stadium witnessed it. Millions more watched it on live television and in the news clips which dominated the agenda for days. John Wilson, a 26-year-old unemployed labourer, clambered over the retaining wall of the main stand and made for Neil Lennon.

Lennon, eyes fixed on the pitch, did not see him coming. 'I felt a contact on the corner of my head and saw a body sprawl in front of me,' Lennon recalled. 'It was then that I realised someone had tried to hit me. I felt like a glancing blow to the corner above the left eye. It all happened very quickly. I went into the defence position to avoid the contact.'

Celtic had just scored their second goal against Hearts. Wilson, who claimed to be on strong painkillers for a football injury to his ribs, had drunk a half bottle of Buckfast and two pints. He was angry, he said, that Lennon had celebrated the goal in front of the home fans.

As he leaped at Lennon he was intercepted by Celtic coach Alan Thompson, who grabbed him as he swung the blow, knocking him off balance so that he slipped on the wet turf.

The Tynecastle security manager Peter Croy leaped on top of Wilson before the police descended. Croy told the jury at Wilson's trial at the end of July that he heard

Wilson call Lennon a 'fenian bastard'. Not true, claimed Wilson, what he actually called him was a 'fucking wanker'.

Wilson was charged with assault and breach of the peace, both aggravated by religious prejudice.

Wilson's trial lawyer was David Nicolson. This is the verbatim transcript of the most crucial part of Wilson's evidence.

Nicolson: Do you accept you ran onto the field of play?
Wilson: Yes.
Nicolson: Do you accept you ran to the away dugout?
Wilson: Yes.
Nicolson: Do you accept you were shouting and swearing?
Wilson: Yes.
Nicolson: Do you accept that caused annoyance to others?
Wilson: Yes.
Nicolson: Do you accept it caused disturbance in the crowd?
Wilson:Yes.
Nicolson: Do you accept you lunged at Neil Lennon?
Wilson: Yes.
Nicolson: Do you accept you assaulted Neil Lennon?

Wilson: Yes.

Nicolson: Do you accept you struck him on the head?

Wilson: Yes.

Nicolson: Did you make a sectarian remark?

Wilson: No

Nicolson: Are you sure about that?

Wilson: Yes.

So, bang to rights as they say on TV.

Well, no.

Wilson had admitted the assault in court, he even tried to plead guilty earlier in his trail if the prosecution removed the the assertion that the attack had been 'aggravated by religious prejudice'. The Crown rejected the offer. Before the jury retired to consider their verdict Wilson's lawyer David Nicolson specifically reminded them of his client's offer to plead guilty to assault.

The jury panel comprised eight men and seven women. They were out for two-and-a-half hours and during their deliberations they asked, once more, to view the video of Wilson's attack, which had been shown on TV screens throughout the world.

As I wrote earlier, Lennon had been the victim of unprecedented attacks on him, assault, bullets in the post, and a parcel bomb (his lawyer Paul McBride QC and former MSP and Celtic fan Trish Godmnan). He was surely more shocked than anyone when the jury returned to deliver their verdict.

Since 1728 in Scotland juries have been given a third legal option in addition to guilty and not guilty – not proven. This verdict counts as an acquittal. It was described by Sir Walter Scott, himself a sheriff, as the 'bastard verdict'. Or as lawyers describe the verdict – 'not guilty but don't do it again!'

The jury pronounced their verdicts. They had struck out the religious prejudice tag on both charges and then found the assault not proven, leaving only the minor conviction for breach of the peace. Wilson was sentenced to eight months in jail but as he had already been held on remand he walked free just weeks later.

The legal establishment was dumbfounded. There could not have been a clearer assault, witnessed not by the two people needed under Scots Law to corroborate an incident, but millions throughout the world.

The Scottish Sun probably summed it up best. Their banner headline over the gigantic picture of the attack read: *So what part of this is NOT an assault on Neil Lennon?*

Lennon's lawyer Paul McBride blasted the contrary verdict. 'What does this say about this country?' he asked. 'It sends out signals to thugs that they can get away with it. The whole world saw the video of the incident. The whole world heard his own counsel admit an attack in court. And now the whole world has seen the jury let him off.

'It is a very dark day for Scottish justice and is a

terrible message about how this country is seen by the rest of the world. I've even had emails from people in America who saw this unfold on the telly and now they're asking how this man could possibly get off.'

Celtic response was measured and graceful in the extreme.

'It is for the jury to decide on this case. However we find the acquittal of the charge of assault difficult to comprehend, bearing in mind our knowledge of the incident.

'One thing is clear – this was a disgraceful incident involving Neil Lennon, seen by the world – the sort of incident which should not have happened in any stadium and one which embarrasses Scottish football.

'Regardless of the verdict reached, we hope that people will learn from the events of last season and realise these cannot be repeated. As always we will give Neil Lennon our full support.'

Paul McBride came back in. 'The jury has acquitted Wilson of a crime he has admitted in open court, namely the assault on Neil Lennon. I am bemused and perplexed by the jury's verdict.

'Neil himself will be apprehensive at work from now on. He is only a human being. If you had been attacked at a place of work you would be anxious about it.'

In the Daily Record I was quoted asking, 'Are we living in Mississippi in the '50s where no one with the wrong colour of skin – or in this case religion – could get justice? This verdict reinforces sectarianism and makes a grotesque mockery of the law.'

There was outrage in the press, and rightly, about the jury verdict which was so obviously contrary to the facts of the case which we all had watched. No one knows exactly what went on in the jury room, because it's an offence to question jurors and for them to describe what must have been negotiations between the 15 members.

In England and Wales juries in criminal cases are directed to reach a unanimous decision and it's only after hours of deliberation and when that can't be reached – a hung jury – that the judge will allow a majority decision. That's not the case in Scotland where a simple majority suffices – indeed people have been actually hanged on it! – as long as eight jurors agree. Anything less is an acquittal.

What the commentariat didn't postulate is this: that a majority of the jury themselves were 'aggravated by religious prejudice'. Unlike what you see in American courtroom dramas Scottish court procedure couldn't be more different. There is not the same scrutiny of prospective jurors, or the elaborate questioning of them prior to the trial with the right of peremptory challenges and exclusions.

As Paul McBride puts it: 'In Scotland, we have juries who do not have to read, who do not have to write and who do not have to count, and may be full of prejudice - unlike other countries.'

Questioning the prospective jurors about their

religion, what teams they followed if any, Masonic association and the like, would have been totally relevant here. It's clear to me that a crucial number of the jury were motivated by religious prejudice and Lennon suffered as a Northern Ireland Catholic, and proud of it. Hence the striking out of the 'aggravation' element of the charge and then the stunning not proven verdict on assault.

If a jury is indeed a representative cross-section of society then by this judgement Scotland is innately prejudiced, bitterly sectarian, unable to dissociate football from religion and totally brazen about it.

We are all shamed.

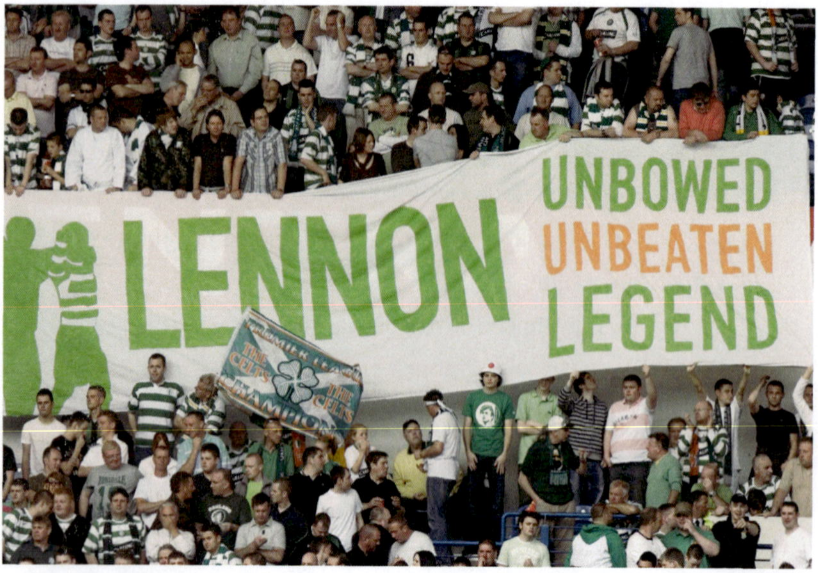
LENNON
UNBOWED
UNBEATEN
LEGEND